The Long Christmas Dinner

And Other Plays in One Act

Books by
THORNTON WILDER

Novels
THE CABALA
THE BRIDGE OF SAN LUIS REY
THE WOMAN OF ANDROS
HEAVEN'S MY DESTINATION
THE IDES OF MARCH

Collections of Short Plays
THE ANGEL THAT TROUBLED THE WATERS
THE LONG CHRISTMAS DINNER

Plays
OUR TOWN
THE MERCHANT OF YONKERS
THE SKIN OF OUR TEETH
THREE PLAYS:
Our Town
The Skin of Our Teeth
The Matchmaker

The Two Worlds of Thornton Wilder

BY JOHN GASSNER

In recommending a volume of short plays by Thornton Wilder published as long ago as 1931 it is tempting to lean on his subsequently achieved reputation as the author of *Our Town* and *The Skin of Our Teeth,* two of the outstanding American plays of the century, and on the fame of several novels since the publication of *The Bridge of San Luis Rey* in 1927 that contain some of the best writing to be found in contemporary American fiction. But the author of these works is interesting to us not as a reputation but as a living artist, and the pleasure derived from the plays in the present volume is sure to be instant and self-sufficient. I trust it is not a momentary judgment of mine that *The Long Christmas Dinner* is the most beautiful one-act play in English prose; at this writing its only rival in my affections is Synge's radically different masterpiece, *Riders to the Sea.*

If *Pullman Car Hiawatha* is bound to suffer by comparison with *Our Town,* it is questionable whether the comparison should be allowed to carry any weight. Since Wilder did not compose the shorter and earlier play as a mere preparatory exercise, it has its own distinct substance and style. The presence of an omniscient Stage Manager in both *Pullman Car Hiawatha* and *Our Town* leaves large areas of difference after the technical resemblance has been duly noted. A third experiment in imaginative theatre, *The Happy Journey to Trenton and Camden,* is a deservedly well-known and frequently performed *tour de force.* And even the conventional realistic dramatic structure of the remaining plays, *Queens of France,* an affecting genre painting of social pretensions in old New Orleans, and *Love and How To Cure It,* a non-stagy glance at stage folk, has unique features gratifying to those who know how to read dramatic literature.

Still, it is within the frame of Wilder's total endeavor as playwright and novelist that these short pieces stand out most meaningfully. And, conversely, these little masterworks help to define their author, concerning whom opinions have been frequently divided and rarely cogent despite the attention paid to his writings and the regard in which he is held on two continents. In this collection of early plays we find (not unexpectedly in the case of so disciplined and self-aware an artist) the configurations of a talent that combines sensitivity with a strong awareness of form and embraces both the commonplaces of life and the life of the imagination, which fluctuates between fantasy and philosophy, skepticism and mysticism, playfulness and sobriety. We see him poised between "life" and "theatre," and this not merely as a beguiling technician but as an observer of

The
Long Christmas Dinner
&
Other Plays in One Act

BY

THORNTON WILDER

HARPER & ROW, PUBLISHERS
NEW YORK, EVANSTON, AND LONDON

Contents

THE TWO WORLDS OF THORNTON WILDER
    BY JOHN GASSNER   vii

THE LONG CHRISTMAS DINNER   1

QUEENS OF FRANCE   29

PULLMAN CAR HIAWATHA   49

LOVE, AND HOW TO CURE IT   71

THE HAPPY JOURNEY TO TRENTON AND
    CAMDEN   89

SELECTED BIBLIOGRAPHY   111

world and was "alarmed at finding a way of cast-
ing into generalization the world of doorbells
and telephones." He was ready, he believed, "to
accept the twentieth century, not only as a fas-
cinating age to live in, but as assimilable stuff to
think with."

He still had to accept the theatre as well. His
first plays, published in 1928 under the collective
title *The Angel That Troubled the Waters,* were
three-minute-long dramatic pieces. They possess
some of the features of a literary conversation in
the manner of Walter Savage Landor but without
Landor's prolixity in prose; there is considerably
less dramatic pressure in them than in the miniature verse plays of Pushkin and the short pieces
Musset wrote to illustrate proverbs. They are ex-
tremely beautiful pieces of writing and I particularly treasure *Now the Servant's Name Was
Malchus* in which "Our Lord" in heaven receives
the servant of the High Priest whose ear was lopped
off by Peter's sword when Christ was arrested.
Malchus would like to have his name expunged
from the New Testament because the episode
makes him look ridiculous. Christ invites him to
stay in heaven with Him, saying, "Malchus, will
you stay and be ridiculous with me?" Malchus says
he will be glad to stay but isn't sure he merits all
that attention: "I wasn't even the High Priest's
servant; I only held his horse every now and then."
Besides, it was his left ear and not his right that
was the casualty of that fateful encounter; where-

upon "Our Lord" assures him that "the book isn't always true about me, either."

The affirmative counterpart to this rather bitter one-acter is another miniature masterpiece, *The Flight into Egypt,* in which Hepzibah, the talkative donkey that carries the Holy Family fleeing from Herod's massacre of the children, loiters dangerously on the road to Egypt. On being ordered to move ahead, Hepzibah reflects that "it's a queer world where the survival of the Lord is dependent on donkeys," and requesting some answers to the puzzle of faith and reason, is told by Our Lady that there will be an answer perhaps someday, but "For the present just do as I do and bear your master on." A third dramatic capsule, *Hast Thou Considered My Servant Job,* asserts faith in man himself. Wilder's often noted optimistic view of man is expressed with unusual warmth when Judas renounces Satan, who has been awaiting his favorite son, confident that he has defeated Christ, "For I build not on intermittent dreams and timid aspirations, but on the unshakable passions and lust and self-love." The stage direction that answers this boast reads: "Suddenly the thirty pieces of silver are cast upward from the revolted hand of Judas. They hurtle across the stars and continue falling forever through the vast funnel of space." Christ and Judas then "mount upward to their due place and Satan remains to this day, uncomprehending, upon the pavement of Hell."

Still, the world of art that Wilder inhabited
with the writing of some forty three-minute plays
(and this activity went as far back as 1915, when
he wrote the first of these in California) was the
same reflective and literary world that had served
him in the novels. It was a strong enticement for
one who had studied the classics in his youth,
written ambitious undergraduate literature, pur-
sued the study of archaeology at the American
Academy in Rome after graduation from Yale in
1920, taught from 1921 to 1928 at the Lawrence-
ville boys' preparatory school near Princeton, and
was to teach again for over half a decade, from 1930
to 1936, at the University of Chicago under the
classically inspired regime of his former Yale class-
mate Robert Hutchins. Characteristically, in writing the Foreword to *The Angel That Troubled
the Waters* in 1928, Wilder declared that "beauty
is the only persuasion." But with the writing of
The Long Christmas Dinner and the other dra-
matically active one-act plays in the present volume
he was plainly intent on achieving something more
than "beauty." He aimed here for the truth of
common life, on the one hand, and its theatrical
expression, on the other.

Henceforth he was to inhabit two worlds, the
real and the imaginary, or to blend the two in
the same work. This was apparent in his later
fiction—in *Heaven's My Destination,* an amusing
yet rueful novel about a moralistic innocent

adrift in American society, published in 1935, and in *The Ides of March* (1948), in which he combined a novel of manners in Julius Caesar's times with a penetrating portrait of Caesar and exquisitively reflective prose often intensified with emotion and lightened with humor. (In the invented letters and diary that make up this semi-Shavian novel one comes across well-turned observations such as Caesar's statements that "The Gods hide themselves even in their choice of instruments," that "Hope has never changed tomorrow's weather," and that "wickedness may be the exploration of one's liberty" and "the search for a limit that one can respect.") But it is especially in the plays published after *The Angel That Troubled the Waters* that Wilder effected the reconciliation of reality and imagination which proved so rewarding in *Our Town* in 1938 and *The Skin of Our Teeth* in 1942.*

* Mr. Wilder, I should add, has been a more prolific playwright since 1931 than the above reference to his major plays would suggest. *The Merchant of Yonkers,* a Max Reinhardt production in 1938, was revised and entitled *The Matchmaker.* In this version the play was produced at the Edinburgh Festival in 1954 and in New York in 1955. He adapted André Obey's poetic drama *Le Viol de Lucrèce* for Katharine Cornell and *A Doll's House* for a Jed Harris presentation featuring Ruth Gordon as Nora, and he wrote an Alcestis drama, *The Alcestiad,* performed at the Edinburgh Festival of 1955 under the title *A Life in the Sun.* Mr. Wilder is now at work on two cycles of one-act plays, *The Seven Ages of Man* and *The Seven Deadly Sins,* from which three pieces were put

To the plays in the present volume belongs the distinction of introducing their author as an original and effective playwright, and three of these will introduce the reader to the essence of his craftsmanship. Thus, the omniscient Stage Manager so important to the structure of *Our Town* first appears in *Pullman Car Hiawatha* and serves the same purpose of introducing the dramatic action and functioning within it. He is both the *raisonneur,* or commentator, and, in speaking the lines of several minor figures, a veritable constellation of characters. The Stage Manager is, so to speak, both a one-man chorus and a multiple "second character," or deuteragonist, in the play, which reflects conventions of both Greek and Oriental drama in this respect while the dialogue and the characterizations are unmistakably American.

Time is telescoped in *The Long Christmas Dinner,* so that ninety years of family life flow through the play without interruption in a sequence of merging scenes. Thornton Wilder was to telescope time again on a more historically significant plane in *The Skin of Our Teeth* a decade later. In *The Long Christmas Dinner* the author's imaginative management of time is simple and

---

together for a Circle-in-the-Square "off-Broadway" production in 1962. In the best of these, *Childhood,* one finds the same fusion of homely reality and piquant fantasy that characterizes the major stage productions.

persuasive. We feel as though we were floating in the flux of life and of time itself, in a broad and never-ending stream which is both "real" and "unreal." We move ahead and are nevertheless becalmed by the sameness of the things that ultimately matter most to us, the quotidian realities that underlie the course of nations and even the ardors and endurances of men and women celebrated in history, saga, and high tragedy. And the marvel is that this effect of simplicity was achieved by the author with some of the most sophisticated strategies of dramaturgy within the competence of modern theatrical art.

The same simplicity of subject and style combined with modernistic structural departures from realism also appears in *The Happy Journey to Trenton and Camden,* in which the author again resorts to a Stage Manager who sets up the visible action and participates in the play in several small roles. In *Pullman Car Hiawatha,* moreover, the author's resources of dramatic construction and symbolic visualization even enable him to move into a world of fancy, allowing him to give a speech to a dead woman (Harriet) as affecting as Emily's lines in the last act of *Our Town* and to personify places such as "Grover's Corners" and "The Field" (too archly, perhaps) in the dramatic action. He even feels free to indulge in the playful histrionics of bringing "The Hours" onstage as "beautiful girls dressed like Elihu Vedder's Pleiades," each carrying a great gold Roman numeral; this, after a whimsical introduction by the Stage Manager to the effect that the minutes are "gossips," the hours "philosophers," and the years "theologians." And following this, anticipating a procession of the hours in *The Skin of Our Teeth*, Ten O'Clock, Eleven O'Clock, and Twelve O'Clock quote Plato, Epictetus, and St. Augustine, while "the planets appear on the balcony." Nothing less than a wistful mysticism relating our insignificant species to the universe satisfies Wilder's imagination once he elects for histrionic freedom or "theatricalism."

It is to be noted, finally, that with this roving kind of dramaturgy he brings us to one more paradoxical attribute of his virtuosity. He is at once a radical and a traditionalist in employing a form of stylization that proclaims the theatrical nature of the drama instead of sedulously sustaining the so-called illusion of reality required by the conventions of modern realism. The artificial nature of the theatre was the established convention of classic, Oriental, Renaissance, Elizabethan, Neoclassic, and Romantic theatre; realistic convention, which became firmly established only in the second half of the nineteenth century, is a very late development. In returning to "theatricalism" or "theatre for theatre's sake" (rather than "theatre for the sake of illusion"), Wilder associated himself with tradition in dramatic art. But returning to tradition in the twentieth century was an innovation, and Wilder's manner of returning to it was personal and unique. It came about not without some dangers, the greatest of these being in his case some frolicsome bookishness and self-conscious skittishness, but it amounted to a minor revolution in the American theatre.

Both its revolutionary character and its risks were, however, minimized by the persuasive humanity, natural tact, and good taste of the well-bred and well-educated author of short and long plays that quickly established themselves as classics of the American theatre in so far as this jittery institution can lay claim to any classics at all. A nearly infallible sense of theatre, moreover, overcame the anti-dramatic tendencies of Thornton Wilder's temperament, giving liveliness to his reflectiveness and life to his artifices. In a little essay entitled *Some Thoughts on Playwriting,* published in 1941, he set down his creed and awareness of craft succinctly. He declared that "the Stage is a fundamental pretense" and that it thrives on the acceptance of that fact and "in the multiplication of additional pretenses." But he went on to affirm the immediacy of life in the drama despite the pretenses of the stage by writing that "A play is what takes place. A novel is what one person tells us took place. A play visibly represents pure existing." He did not have to defend the paradox as his own plays, beginning with *The*

Long Christmas Dinner in 1931, provided suffi-
cient proof of its truth and gratifying results.*

* Readers curious enough about the nature and justi-
fication of this paradox, this dual character of dramatic
art, may refer to the following paragraph in John Gass-
ner's *Form and Idea in Modern Theatre* (pp. 141-42):

> The fundamental premise of realism is the Aris-
> totelian one that drama is an imitation of an action;
> realists held, therefore, that the most desirable theatre
> is that in which imitation is closest. The fundamental
> premise of theatricalism is that theatre is not imita-
> tion in the narrow sense, which Aristotle never could
> have held, since the Greek drama upon which he based
> conclusions in his *Poetics* was not realistically imita-
> tive. For the theatricalist, the object of action and of
> all other 'imitative' elements is not imitation but cre-
> ativeness, and a special kind of creativeness at that.
> The realists would agree, of course, as to the value of
> creativeness. But the theatricalist goes one step fur-
> ther, and that step is the truly decisive one for the
> theory and practice of pure theatricalism. He main-
> tains that there is never any sense in pretending that
> one is not in the theatre; that no amount of make-
> believe is reality itself; that in short, theatre is the
> medium of dramatic art, and that effectiveness in art
> consists in *using* the medium rather than concealing it.

And Thornton Wilder provided conclusive evidence
of the compatibility of convention and emotional conviction with an example in *Some Thoughts on Playwriting*.
Starting with the statement that the theatre "lives by
conventions: a convention is an agreed-upon falsehood,
a permitted lie," he cited the case of Euripides' *Medea*.
According to an ancient report, the passage in the play
where Medea contemplates the murder of her children
nearly produced a riot. Yet Medea was "played by a
man," "he wore a large mask on his face," "he wore shoes
with soles and heels half a foot high," he spoke in metric

lines and "all poetry is an 'agreed-upon falsehood' in regard to speech," and "the lines were sung in a kind of recitative"—as in opera, which "involves this 'permitted lie' in regard to speech." Wilder rightly concluded that the mask, the costume, and the mode of declamation were "a series of signs which the spectator interpreted and reassembled in his own mind." That is, "Medea was being recreated within the imagination of each of the spectators."

The Long Christmas Dinner

And Other Plays in One Act

The Long Christmas Dinner

The dining-room of the Bayard home. Close to the footlights a long dining table is handsomely spread for Christmas dinner. The carver's place with a great turkey before it is at the spectator's right.

A door, left back, leads into the hall.

At the extreme left, by the proscenium pillar, is a strange portal trimmed with garlands of fruits and flowers. Directly opposite is another edged and hung with black velvet. The portals denote birth and death.

Ninety years are to be traversed in this play which represents in accelerated motion ninety Christmas dinners in the Bayard household. The actors are dressed in inconspicuous clothes and must indicate their gradual increase in years through their acting. Most of them carry wigs of white hair which they adjust upon their heads at the indicated moment, simply and without comment. The ladies may have shawls concealed beneath the table that they gradually draw up about their shoulders as they grow older.

Throughout the play the characters continue eating imaginary food with imaginary knives and forks.

There is no curtain. The audience arriving at the theatre sees the stage set and the table laid,

though still in partial darkness. Gradually the lights in the auditorium become dim and the stage brightens until sparkling winter sunlight streams through the dining room windows.
Enter Lucia. She inspects the table, touching here a knife and there a fork. She talks to a servant girl who is invisible to us.

LUCIA. I reckon we're ready now, Gertrude. We won't ring the chimes today. I'll just call them myself.

She goes into the hall and calls:
Roderick. Mother Bayard. We're all ready. Come to dinner.

Enter Roderick pushing Mother Bayard in a wheel chair.

MOTHER BAYARD. . . . and a new horse too, Roderick. I used to think that only the wicked owned two horses. A new horse and a new house and a new wife!

RODERICK. Well, Mother, how do you like it? Our first Christmas dinner in the new house, hey?

MOTHER BAYARD. Tz-Tz-Tz! I don't know what your dear father would say!

LUCIA. Here, Mother Bayard, you sit between us.

Roderick *says grace.*

MOTHER BAYARD. My dear Lucia, I can remember when there were still Indians on this very ground, and I wasn't a young girl either. I can remember when we had to cross the Mississippi on a new-made raft. I can remember when St. Louis and Kansas City were full of Indians.

LUCIA (*tying a napkin around* Mother Bayard's *neck*). Imagine that! There!—What a wonderful day for our first Christmas dinner: a beautiful sunny morning, snow, a splendid sermon. Dr. McCarthy preaches a splendid sermon. I cried and cried.

RODERICK (*extending an imaginary carving-fork*). Come now, what'll you have, Mother? A little sliver of white?

LUCIA. Every least twig is wrapped around with ice. You almost never see that. Can I cut it up for you, dear? (*over her shoulder*) Gertrude, I forgot the jelly. You know,—on the top shelf.— Mother Bayard, I found your mother's gravy-boat while we were moving. What was her name, dear? What were all your names? You were . . . a . . . Genevieve Wainright. Now your mother—

MOTHER BAYARD. Yes, you must write it down somewhere. I was Genevieve Wainright. My mother was Faith Morrison. She was the daughter of a farmer in New Hampshire who was something of a blacksmith too. And she married young John Wainright—

LUCIA (*memorizing on her fingers*). Genevieve Wainright. Faith Morrison.

RODERICK. It's all down in a book somewhere upstairs. We have it all. All that kind of thing is very interesting. Come, Lucia, just a little wine. Mother, a little red wine for Christmas day. Full of iron. "Take a little wine for thy stomach's sake."

LUCIA. Really, I can't get used to wine! What would my father say? But I suppose it's all right.

Enter Cousin Brandon *from the hall. He takes his place by* Lucia.

COUSIN BRANDON (*rubbing his hands*). Well, well, I smell turkey. My dear cousins, I can't tell you how pleasant it is to be having Christmas dinner with you all. I've lived out there in Alaska so long without relatives. Let me see, how long have you had this new house, Roderick?

RODERICK. Why, it must be . . .

MOTHER BAYARD. Five years. It's five years, children. You should keep a diary. This is your sixth Christmas dinner here.

LUCIA. Think of that, Roderick. We feel as though we had lived here twenty years.

COUSIN BRANDON. At all events it still looks as good as new.

RODERICK (*over his carving*). What'll you have, Brandon, light or dark?—Frieda, fill up Cousin Brandon's glass.

LUCIA. Oh, dear, I can't get used to these wines. I don't know what my father'd say, I'm sure. What'll you have, Mother Bayard?

During the following speeches Mother Bayard's *chair, without any visible propulsion, starts to draw away from the table, turns toward the right, and slowly goes toward the dark portal.*

MOTHER BAYARD. Yes, I can remember when there were Indians on this very land.

LUCIA (*softly*). Mother Bayard hasn't been very well lately, Roderick.

MOTHER BAYARD. My mother was a Faith Morrison. And in New Hampshire she married a young John Wainright, who was a Congregational minister. He saw her in his congregation one day . . .

LUCIA. Mother Bayard, hadn't you better lie down, dear?

MOTHER BAYARD. . . . and right in the middle of his sermon he said to himself: "I'll marry that girl." And he did, and I'm their daughter.

LUCIA (*half rising and looking after her with anxiety*). Just a little nap, dear?

MOTHER BAYARD. I'm all right. Just go on with your dinner. I was ten, and I said to my brother—

She goes out. A very slight pause.

COUSIN BRANDON. It's too bad it's such a cold dark day today. We almost need the lamps. I spoke to Major Lewis for a moment after church. His sciatica troubles him, but he does pretty well.

LUCIA (*dabbing her eyes*). I know Mother Bayard wouldn't want us to grieve for her on Christmas day, but I can't forget her sitting in her wheel chair right beside us, only a year ago. And she would be so glad to know our good news.

RODERICK (*patting her hand*). Now, now. It's Christmas. (*formally*) Cousin Brandon, a glass of wine with you, sir.

COUSIN BRANDON (*half rising, lifting his glass gallantly*). A glass of wine with you, sir.

LUCIA. Does the Major's sciatica cause him much pain?

COUSIN BRANDON. Some, perhaps. But you know his way. He says it'll be all the same in a hundred years.

LUCIA. Yes, he's a great philosopher.

RODERICK. His wife sends you a thousand thanks for her Christmas present.

LUCIA. I forget what I gave her.—Oh, yes, the workbasket!

> *Through the entrance of birth comes a nurse wheeling a perambulator trimmed with blue ribbons.* Lucia *rushes toward it, the men following.*

O my wonderful new baby, my darling baby! Who ever saw such a child! Quick, nurse, a boy or a girl? A boy! Roderick, what shall we call him? Really, nurse, you've never seen such a child!

RODERICK. We'll call him Charles after your father and grandfather.

LUCIA. But there are no Charleses in the Bible, Roderick.

RODERICK. Of course, there are. Surely there are.

LUCIA. Roderick!—Very well, but he will always be Samuel to me.—What miraculous hands he has! Really, they are the most beautiful hands in the world. All right, nurse. Have a good nap, my darling child.

RODERICK. Don't drop him, nurse. Brandon and I need him in our firm.

Exit nurse and perambulator into the hall. The others return to their chairs, Lucia *taking the place left vacant by* Mother Bayard *and* Cousin Brandon *moving up beside her.* Cousin Brandon *puts on his white hair.*

Lucia, a little white meat? Some stuffing? Cranberry sauce, anybody?

LUCIA (*over her shoulder*). Margaret, the stuffing is very good today.—Just a little, thank you.

RODERICK. Now something to wash it down. (*half rising*) Cousin Brandon, a glass of wine with you, sir. To the ladies, God bless them.

LUCIA. Thank you, kind sirs.

COUSIN BRANDON. Pity it's such an overcast day today. And no snow.

LUCIA. But the sermon was lovely. I cried and cried. Dr. Spaulding does preach such a splendid sermon.

RODERICK. I saw Major Lewis for a moment after church. He says his rheumatism comes and goes. His wife says she has something for Charles and will bring it over this afternoon.

Enter nurse again with perambulator. Pink ribbons. Same rush toward the left.

LUCIA. O my lovely new baby! Really, it never occurred to me that it might be a girl. Why, nurse, she's perfect.

RODERICK. Now call her what you choose. It's your turn.

LUCIA. Looloolooloo. Aië. Aië. Yes, this time I shall have my way. She shall be called Genevieve after your mother. Have a good nap, my treasure.

She looks after it as the nurse wheels the perambulator into the hall.

Imagine! Sometime she'll be grown up and say "Good morning, Mother. Good morning, Father." —Really, Cousin Brandon, you don't find a baby like that every day.

COUSIN BRANDON. *And* the new factory.

LUCIA. A new factory? Really? Roderick, I shall be very uncomfortable if we're going to turn out to be rich. I've been afraid of that for years.— However, we mustn't talk about such things on Christmas day. I'll just take a little piece of white meat, thank you. Roderick, Charles is destined for the ministry. I'm sure of it.

RODERICK. Woman, he's only twelve. Let him have a free mind. *We* want him in the firm, I don't mind saying. Anyway, no time passes as slowly as this when you're waiting for your urchins to grow up and settle down to business.

LUCIA. I don't want time to go any faster, thank you. I love the children just as they are.—Really, Roderick, you know what the doctor said: One glass a meal. (*putting her hand over his glass*) No, Margaret, that will be all.

Roderick *rises, glass in hand. With a look of*

dismay on his face he takes a few steps toward the dark portal.

RODERICK. Now I wonder what's the matter with me.

LUCIA. Roderick, do be reasonable.

RODERICK (*tottering, but with gallant irony*). But, my dear, statistics show that we steady, moderate drinkers . . .

LUCIA (*rises, gazing at him in anguish*). Roderick! My dear! What . . .?

RODERICK (*returns to his seat with a frightened look of relief*). Well, it's fine to be back at table with you again. How many good Christmas dinners have I had to miss upstairs? And to be back at a fine bright one, too.

LUCIA. O my dear, you gave us a very alarming time! Here's your glass of milk.—Josephine, bring Mr. Bayard his medicine from the cupboard in the library.

RODERICK. At all events, now that I'm better I'm going to start doing something about the house.

LUCIA. Roderick! You're not going to change the house?

RODERICK. Only touch it up here and there. It looks a hundred years old.

Charles *enters casually from the hall. He kisses his mother's hair and sits down.*

LUCIA. Charles, you carve the turkey, dear. Your father's not well.—You always said you hated carving, though you *are* so clever at it.

Father and son exchange places.

CHARLES. It's a great blowy morning, mother. The wind comes over the hill like a lot of cannon.

LUCIA. And such a good sermon. I cried and cried. Mother Bayard loved a good sermon so. And she used to sing the Christmas hymns all around the year. Oh, dear, oh, dear, I've been thinking of her all morning!

RODERICK. Sh, Mother. It's Christmas day. You mustn't think of such things.—You mustn't be depressed.

LUCIA. But sad things aren't the same as depressing things. I must be getting old: I like them.

CHARLES. Uncle Brandon, you haven't anything to eat. Pass his plate, Hilda . . . and some cranberry sauce . . .

Enter Genevieve. *She kisses her father's temple and sits down.*

GENEVIEVE. It's glorious. Every least twig is wrapped around with ice. You almost never see that.

LUCIA. Did you have time to deliver those presents after church, Genevieve?

GENEVIEVE. Yes, Mama. Old Mrs. Lewis sends you a thousand thanks for hers. It was just what she wanted, she said. Give me lots, Charles, lots.

RODERICK (*rising and starting toward the dark portal*). Statistics, ladies and gentlemen, show that we steady, moderate . . .

CHARLES. How about a little skating this afternoon, Father?

RODERICK. I'll live till I'm ninety.

LUCIA. I really don't think he ought to go skating.

RODERICK (*at the very portal, suddenly astonished*). Yes, but . . . but . . . not yet!

He goes out.

LUCIA (*dabbing her eyes*). He was so young and so clever, Cousin Brandon. (*raising her voice for* Cousin Brandon's *deafness*) I say he was so young and so clever.—Never forget your father, children. He was a good man.—Well, he wouldn't want us to grieve for him today.

CHARLES. White or dark, Genevieve? Just another sliver, Mother?

LUCIA (*putting on her white hair*). I can remember our first Christmas dinner in this house, Genevieve. Twenty-five years ago today. Mother Bayard was sitting here in her wheel chair. She could remember when Indians lived on this very spot and when she had to cross the river on a new-made raft.

CHARLES AND GENEVIEVE. She couldn't have, Mother. That can't be true.

LUCIA. It certainly was true—even I can remember when there was only one paved street. We were very happy to walk on boards. (*louder, to* Cousin Brandon) We can remember when there were no sidewalks, can't we, Cousin Brandon?

COUSIN BRANDON (*delighted*). Oh, yes! And those were the days.

CHARLES AND GENEVIEVE (*sotto voce. This is a family refrain*). Those were the days.

LUCIA. . . . and the ball last night, Genevieve? Did you have a nice time? I hope you didn't *waltz,* dear. I think a girl in our position ought to set an example. Did Charles keep an eye on you?

GENEVIEVE. He had none left. They were all on Leonora Banning. He can't conceal it any longer, Mother. I think he's engaged to marry Leonora Banning.

CHARLES. I'm not engaged to marry anyone.

LUCIA. Well, she's very pretty.

GENEVIEVE. I shall never marry, Mother—I shall sit in this house beside you forever, as though life were one long, happy Christmas dinner.

LUCIA. O my child, you mustn't say such things!

GENEVIEVE (*playfully*). You don't want me? You don't want me?

Lucia *bursts into tears.*

Why, Mother, how silly you are! There's nothing sad about that—what could possibly be sad about that.

LUCIA (*drying her eyes*). Forgive me. I'm just unpredictable, that's all.

Charles *goes to the door and leads in* Leonora Banning.

LEONORA (*kissing* Lucia's *temple*). Good morning, Mother Bayard. Good morning, everybody. It's really a splendid Christmas day today.

CHARLES. Little white meat? Genevieve, Mother, Leonora?

LEONORA. Every least twig is encircled with ice.—You never see that.

CHARLES (*shouting*). Uncle Brandon, another? —Rogers, fill my uncle's glass.

LUCIA (*to Charles*). Do what your father used to do. It would please Cousin Brandon so. You know—(*pretending to raise a glass*)—"Uncle Brandon, a glass of wine—"

CHARLES (*rising*). Uncle Brandon, a glass of wine with you, sir.

BRANDON. A glass of wine with you, sir. To the ladies, God bless them every one.

THE LADIES. Thank you, kind sirs.

GENEVIEVE. And if I go to Germany for my music I promise to be back for Christmas. I wouldn't miss that.

LUCIA. I hate to think of you over there all alone in those strange pensions.

GENEVIEVE. But, darling, the time will pass so fast that you'll hardly know I'm gone. I'll be back in the twinkling of an eye.

Enter Left, the nurse and perambulator. Green ribbons.

LEONORA. Oh, what an angel! The darlingest baby in the world. Do let me hold it, nurse.

But the nurse resolutely wheels the perambulator across the stage and out the dark door.

Oh, I did love it so!

> Lucia *goes to her, puts her arm around* Leonora's *shoulders, and they encircle the room whispering*—Lucia *then hands her over to* Charles *who conducts her on the same circuit.*

GENEVIEVE (*as her mother sits down,—softly*). Isn't there anything I can do?

LUCIA (*raises her eyebrows, ruefully*). No, dear. Only time, only the passing of time can help in these things.

> Charles *and* Leonora *return to the table.*

Don't you think we could ask Cousin Ermengarde to come and live with us here? There's plenty for everyone and there's no reason why she should go on teaching the First Grade for ever and ever. She wouldn't be in the way, would she, Charles?

CHARLES. No, I think it would be fine.—A little more potato and gravy, anybody? A little more turkey, Mother?

> Brandon *rises and starts slowly toward the dark portal.*
>
> Lucia *rises and stands for a moment with her face in her hands.*

COUSIN BRANDON (*muttering*). It was great to be in Alaska in those days . . .

GENEVIEVE (*half rising, and gazing at her mother in fear*). Mother, what is . . .?

LUCIA (*hurriedly*). Hush, my dear. It will pass. —Hold fast to your music, you know. (*as Gene-*

vieve *starts toward her*) No, no. I want to be alone for a few minutes.

> *She turns and starts after* Cousin Brandon *toward the Right.*

CHARLES. If the Republicans collected all their votes instead of going off into cliques among themselves, they might prevent his getting a second term.

GENEVIEVE. Charles, Mother doesn't tell us, but she hasn't been very well these days.

CHARLES. Come, Mother, we'll go to Florida for a few weeks.

> *Exit* Brandon.

LUCIA (*smiling at* Genevieve *and waving her hand*). Don't be foolish. Don't grieve.

> *She clasps her hands under her chin; her lips move, whispering; she walks serenely into the portal.*
>
> Genevieve *stares after her, frozen.*
>
> *At the same moment the nurse and perambulator enter from the Left. Pale yellow ribbons.* Leonora *rushes to it.*

LEONORA. O my darlings . . . twins . . . Charles, aren't they glorious! Look at them. Look at them.

GENEVIEVE (*sinks down on the table her face buried in her arms*). But what will I do? What's left for me to do?

CHARLES (*bending over the basket*). Which is which?

LEONORA. I feel as though I were the first

mother who ever had twins.—Look at them now!
—But why wasn't Mother Bayard allowed to stay
and see them!

GENEVIEVE (*rising suddenly distraught, loudly*).
I don't want to go on. I can't bear it.

CHARLES (*goes to her quickly. They sit down.
He whispers to her earnestly taking both her
hands*). But Genevieve, Genevieve! How fright-
fully Mother would feel to think that . . . Genevieve!

GENEVIEVE (*shaking her head wildly*). I never
told her how wonderful she was. We all treated
her as though she were just a friend in the house.
I thought she'd be here forever.

LEONORA (*timidly*). Genevieve darling, do
come one minute and hold my babies' hands. We
shall call the girl Lucia after her grandmother,—
will that please you? Do just see what adorable
little hands they have.

> Genevieve *collects herself and goes over to
> the perambulator. She smiles brokenly into
> the basket.*

GENEVIEVE. They are wonderful, Leonora.

LEONORA. Give him your finger, darling. Just
let him hold it.

CHARLES. And we'll call the boy Samuel.—Well,
now everybody come and finish your dinners.
Don't drop them, nurse; at least don't drop the
boy. We need him in the firm.

LEONORA (*stands looking after them as the
nurse wheels them into the hall*). Someday they'll

be big. Imagine! They'll come in and say "Hello, Mother!" (*She makes clucking noises of rapturous consternation.*)

CHARLES. Come, a little wine, Leonora, Genevieve? Full of iron. Eduardo, fill the ladies' glasses. It certainly is a keen, cold morning. I used to go skating with Father on mornings like this and Mother would come back from church saying—

GENEVIEVE (*dreamily*). I know: saying "Such a splendid sermon. I cried and cried."

LEONORA. Why did she cry, dear?

GENEVIEVE. That generation all cried at sermons. It was their way.

LEONORA. Really, Genevieve?

GENEVIEVE. They had had to go since they were children and I suppose sermons reminded them of their fathers and mothers, just as Christmas dinners do us. Especially in an old house like this.

LEONORA. It really is pretty old, Charles. And so ugly, with all that ironwork filigree and that dreadful cupola.

GENEVIEVE. Charles! You aren't going to change the house!

CHARLES. No, no. I won't give up the house, but great heavens! it's fifty years old. This Spring we'll remove the cupola and build a new wing toward the tennis courts.

From now on Genevieve *is seen to change. She sits up more straightly. The corners of*

*her mouth become fixed. She becomes a
forthright and slightly disillusioned spinster.
Charles becomes the plain business man and
a little pompous.*

LEONORA. And then couldn't we ask your dear
old Cousin Ermengarde to come and live with
us? She's really the self-effacing kind.

CHARLES. Ask her now. Take her out of the
First Grade.

GENEVIEVE. We only seem to think of it on
Christmas day with her Christmas card staring us
in the face.

*Enter Left, nurse and perambulator. Blue
ribbons.*

LEONORA. Another boy! Another boy! Here's
a Roderick for you at last.

CHARLES. Roderick Brandon Bayard. A regular
little fighter.

LEONORA. Goodbye, darling. Don't grow up
too fast. Yes, yes. Aië, aië, aië—stay just as you
are.—Thank you, nurse.

GENEVIEVE (*who has not left the table, repeats
dryly*). Stay just as you are.

*Exit nurse and perambulator. The others
return to their places.*

LEONORA. Now I have three children. One, two,
three. Two boys and a girl. I'm collecting them.
It's very exciting. (*over her shoulder*) What,
Hilda? Oh, Cousin Ermengarde's come! Come in,
Cousin.

She goes to the hall and welcomes Cousin

Ermengarde *who already wears her white hair.*

ERMENGARDE (*shyly*). It's such a pleasure to be with you all.

CHARLES (*pulling out her chair for her*). The twins have taken a great fancy to you already, Cousin.

LEONORA. The baby went to her at once.

CHARLES. Exactly how are we related, Cousin Ermengarde?—There, Genevieve, that's your specialty.—First a little more turkey and stuffing, Mother? Cranberry sauce, anybody?

GENEVIEVE. I can work it out: Grandmother Bayard was your . . .

ERMENGARDE. Your Grandmother Bayard was a second cousin of my Grandmother Haskins through the Wainrights.

CHARLES. Well, it's all in a book somewhere upstairs. All that kind of thing is awfully interesting.

GENEVIEVE. Nonsense. There are no such books. I collect my notes off gravestones, and you have to scrape a good deal of moss—let me tell you—to find one great-grandparent.

CHARLES. There's a story that my Grandmother Bayard crossed the Mississippi on a raft before there were any bridges or ferryboats. She died before Genevieve or I were born. Time certainly goes very fast in a great new country like this. Have some more cranberry sauce, Cousin Ermengarde.

ERMENGARDE (*timidly*). Well, time must be passing very slowly in Europe with this dreadful, dreadful war going on.

CHARLES. Perhaps an occasional war isn't so bad after all. It clears up a lot of poisons that collect in nations. It's like a boil.

ERMENGARDE. Oh, dear, oh, dear!

CHARLES (*with relish*). Yes, it's like a boil.— Ho! ho! Here are your twins.

The twins appear at the door into the hall. Sam is wearing the uniform of an ensign. Lucia is fussing over some detail on it.

LUCIA. Isn't he wonderful in it, Mother?

CHARLES. Let's get a look at you.

SAM. Mother, don't let Roderick fool with my stamp album while I'm gone.

LEONORA. Now, Sam, do write a letter once in a while. Do be a good boy about that, mind.

SAM. You might send some of those cakes of yours once in a while, Cousin Ermengarde.

ERMENGARDE (*in a flutter*). I certainly will, my dear boy.

CHARLES. If you need any money, we have agents in Paris and London, remember.

SAM. Well, goodbye . . .

Sam goes briskly out through the dark portal, tossing his unneeded white hair through the door before him.

Lucia sits down at the table with lowered eyes.

ERMENGARDE (*after a slight pause, in a low, constrained voice, making conversation*). I spoke to Mrs. Fairchild for a moment coming out of church. Her rheumatism's a little better, she says. She sends you her warmest thanks for the Christmas present. The workbasket, wasn't it?—It was an admirable sermon. And our stained-glass window looked so beautiful, Leonora, so beautiful. Everybody spoke of it and so affectionately of Sammy. (Leonora's *hand goes to her mouth.*) Forgive me, Leonora, but it's better to speak of him than not to speak of him when we're all thinking of him so hard.

LEONORA (*rising, in anguish*). He was a mere boy. He was a mere boy, Charles.

CHARLES. My dear, my dear.

LEONORA. I want to tell him how wonderful he was. We let him go so casually. I want to tell him how we all feel about him.—Forgive me, let me walk about a minute.—Yes, of course, Ermengarde—it's best to speak of him.

LUCIA (*in a low voice to Genevieve*). Isn't there anything I can do?

GENEVIEVE. No, no. Only time, only the passing of time can help in these things.

Leonora, *straying about the room finds herself near the door to the hall at the moment that her son* Roderick *enters. He links his arm with hers and leads her back to the table.*

RODERICK. What's the matter, anyway? What

are you all so glum about? The skating was fine today.

CHARLES. Sit down, young man. I have something to say to you.

RODERICK. Everybody was there. Lucia skated in the corners with Dan Creighton the whole time. When'll it be, Lucia, when'll it be?

LUCIA. I don't know what you mean.

RODERICK. Lucia's leaving us soon, Mother. Dan Creighton, of all people.

CHARLES (*ominously*). Roderick, I have something to say to you.

RODERICK. Yes, Father.

CHARLES. Is it true, Roderick, that you made yourself conspicuous last night at the Country Club—at a Christmas Eve dance, too?

LEONORA. Not now, Charles, I beg of you. This is Christmas dinner.

RODERICK (*loudly*). No, I didn't.

LUCIA. Really, Father, he didn't. It was that dreadful Johnny Lewis.

CHARLES. I don't want to hear about Johnny Lewis. I want to know whether a son of mine . . .

LEONORA. Charles, I beg of you . . .

CHARLES. The first family of this city!

RODERICK (*rising*). I hate this town and everything about it. I always did.

CHARLES. You behaved like a spoiled puppy, sir, an ill-bred spoiled puppy.

RODERICK. What did I do? What did I do that was wrong?

CHARLES. You were drunk and you were rude to the daughters of my best friends.

GENEVIEVE (*striking the table*). Nothing in the world deserves an ugly scene like this. Charles, I'm ashamed of you.

RODERICK. Great God, you gotta get drunk in this town to forget how dull it is. Time passes so slowly here that it stands still, that's what's the trouble.

CHARLES. Well, young man, we can employ your time. You will leave the university and you will come into the Bayard factory on January second.

RODERICK (*at the door into the hall*). I have better things to do than to go into your old factory. I'm going somewhere where time passes, my God!

He goes out into the hall.

LEONORA (*rising*). Roderick, Roderick, come here just a moment.—Charles where can he go?

LUCIA (*rising*). Sh, Mother. He'll come back. Now I have to go upstairs and pack my trunk.

LEONORA. I won't have any children left!

LUCIA. Sh, Mother. He'll come back. He's only gone to California or somewhere.—Cousin Ermengarde has done most of my packing—thanks a thousand times, Cousin Ermengarde. (*She kisses her mother.*) I won't be long.

She runs out into the hall.

Genevieve *and* Leonora *put on their white hair.*

ERMENGARDE. It's a very beautiful day. On the way home from church I stopped and saw Mrs. Foster a moment. Her arthritis comes and goes.

LEONORA. Is she actually in pain, dear?

ERMENGARDE. Oh, she says it'll all be the same in a hundred years!

LEONORA. Yes, she's a brave little stoic.

CHARLES. Come now, a little white meat, Mother?—Mary, pass my cousin's plate.

LEONORA. What is it, Mary?—Oh, here's a telegram from them in Paris! "Love and Christmas greetings to all." I told them we'd be eating some of their wedding cake and thinking about them today. It seems to be all decided that they will settle down in the East, Ermengarde. I can't even have my daughter for a neighbor. They hope to build before long somewhere on the shore north of New York.

GENEVIEVE. There is no shore north of New York.

LEONORA. Well, East or West or whatever it is.
Pause.

CHARLES. My, what a dark day.
He puts on his white hair. Pause.
How slowly time passes without any young people in the house.

LEONORA. I have three children somewhere.

CHARLES (*blunderingly offering comfort*). Well, one of them gave his life for his country.

LEONORA (*sadly*). And one of them is selling aluminum in China.

GENEVIEVE (*slowly working herself up to a hysterical crisis*). I can stand everything but this terrible soot everywhere. We should have moved long ago. We're surrounded by factories. We have to change the window curtains every week.

LEONORA. Why, Genevieve!

GENEVIEVE. I can't stand it. I can't stand it any more. I'm going abroad. It's not only the soot that comes through the very walls of this house; it's the *thoughts,* it's the thought of what has been and what might have been here. And the feeling about this house of the years *grinding away.* My mother died yesterday—not twenty-five years ago. Oh, I'm going to live and die abroad! Yes, I'm going to be the American old maid living and dying in a pension in Munich or Florence.

ERMENGARDE. Genevieve, you're tired.

CHARLES. Come, Genevieve, take a good drink of cold water. Mary, open the window a minute.

GENEVIEVE. I'm sorry. I'm sorry.

She hurries tearfully out into the hall.

ERMENGARDE. Dear Genevieve will come back to us, I think.

She rises and starts toward the dark portal.

You should have been out today, Leonora. It was one of those days when everything was encircled with ice. Very pretty, indeed.

Charles rises and starts after her.

CHARLES. Leonora, I used to go skating with Father on mornings like this.—I wish I felt a little better.

LEONORA. What! Have I got two invalids on my hands at once? Now, Cousin Ermengarde, you must get better and help me nurse Charles.

ERMENGARDE. I'll do my best.

Ermengarde *turns at the very portal and comes back to the table.*

CHARLES. Well, Leonora, I'll do what you ask. I'll write the puppy a letter of forgiveness and apology. It's Christmas day. I'll cable it. That's what I'll do.

He goes out the dark door.

LEONORA (*drying her eyes*). Ermengarde, it's such a comfort having you here with me. Mary, I really can't eat anything. Well, perhaps, a sliver of white meat.

ERMENGARDE (*very old*). I spoke to Mrs. Keene for a moment coming out of church. She asked after the young people.—At church I felt very proud sitting under our windows, Leonora, and our brass tablets. The Bayard aisle,—it's a regular Bayard aisle and I love it.

LEONORA. Ermengarde, would you be very angry with me if I went and stayed with the young people a little this Spring?

ERMENGARDE. Why, no. I know how badly they want you and need you. Especially now that they're about to build a new house.

LEONORA. You wouldn't be angry? This house is yours as long as you want it, remember.

ERMENGARDE. I don't see why the rest of you dislike it. I like it more than I can say.

LEONORA. I won't be long. I'll be back in no time and we can have some more of our readings-aloud in the evening.

She kisses her and goes into the hall. Ermengarde *left alone, eats slowly and talks to* Mary.

ERMENGARDE. Really, Mary, I'll change my mind. If you'll ask Bertha to be good enough to make me a little eggnog. A dear little eggnog. —Such a nice letter this morning from Mrs. Bayard, Mary. Such a nice letter. They're having their first Christmas dinner in the new house. They must be very happy. They call her Mother Bayard, she says, as though she were an old lady. And she says she finds it more comfortable to come and go in a wheel chair.—Such a dear letter. . . . And Mary, I can tell you a secret. It's still a great secret, mind! They're expecting a grand-child. Isn't that good news! Now I'll read a little.

She props a book up before her, still dipping a spoon into a custard from time to time.
She grows from very old to immensely old.
She sighs. The book falls down. She finds a cane beside her, and soon totters into the dark portal, murmuring:
"Dear little Roderick and little Lucia."

THE END

Queens of France

❧❧❧❧❧❧❧❧❧❧❧❧❧❧❧❧❧❧❧❧❧❧❧❧❧❧❧

A lawyer's office in New Orleans, 1869.

The door to the street is hung with a reed curtain, through which one obtains a glimpse of a public park in sunshine.

A small bell tinkles. After a pause it rings again.

Marie-Sidonie Cressaux *pushes the reeds apart and peers in. She is an attractive young woman equal to any situation in life except a summons to a lawyer's office.*

M'su Cahusac, *a dry little man with sharp black eyes, enters from an inner room.*

MARIE-SIDONIE (*indicating a letter in her hand*). You . . . you have asked me to come and see you.

M. CAHUSAC (*severe and brief*). Your name, Madame?

MARIE-SIDONIE. Mamselle Marie-Sidonie Cressaux, M'su.

M. CAHUSAC (*after a pause*). Yes. Kindly be seated, Mamselle.

> *He goes to his desk and opens a great many drawers, collecting documents from each. Presently having assembled a large bundle he returns to the center of the room and says abruptly:*

Mamselle, this interview is to be regarded by you as strictly confidential.

MARIE-SIDONIE. Yes, M'su.

M. CAHUSAC (*after looking at her sternly a moment*). May I ask if Mamselle is able to bear the shock of surprise, of good or bad news?

MARIE-SIDONIE. Why . . . yes, M'su.

M. CAHUSAC. Then if you are Mamselle Marie-Sidonie Cressaux, the daughter of Baptiste-Anténor Cressaux, it is my duty to inform you that you are in danger.

MARIE-SIDONIE. I am in danger, M'su?

He returns to his desk, opens further drawers, and returns with more papers. She follows him with bewildered eyes.

M. CAHUSAC. Mamselle, in addition to my duties as a lawyer in this city, I am the representative here of a Historical Society in Paris. Will you please try and follow me, Mamselle? This Historical Society has been engaged in tracing the descendants of the true heir to the French throne. As you know, at the time of the Revolution, in 1795, to be exact, Mamselle, the true, lawful, and legitimate heir to the French throne disappeared. It was rumored that this boy, who was then ten years old, came to America and lived for a time in New Orleans. We now know that the rumor was true. We now know that he here begot legitimate issue, that this legitimate issue in turn begot legitimate issue, and that—(Marie-Sidonie *suddenly starts searching for something in her shopping bag.*) Mamselle, may I have the honor of your attention a little longer?

MARIE-SIDONIE (*choking*). My fan—my, my fan,

M'su. (*She finds it and at once begins to fan her-self wildly. Suddenly she cries out*): M'su, what danger am I in?

M. CAHUSAC (*sternly*). If Mamselle will exer-cise a moment's—one moment's—patience, she will know all. . . . That legitimate issue here begot legitimate issue, and the royal line of France has been traced to a certain (*he consults his docu-ments*) Baptiste-Anténor Cressaux.

MARIE-SIDONIE (*Her fan stops and she stares at him*). Ba't—ba'tiste . . . !

M. CAHUSAC (*leaning forward with menacing emphasis*). Mamselle, can you *prove* that you are the daughter of Baptiste-Anténor Cressaux?

MARIE-SIDONIE. Why . . . Why . . .

M. CAHUSAC. Mamselle, have you a certificate of your parents' marriage?

MARIE-SIDONIE. Yes, M'su.

M. CAHUSAC. If it turns out to be valid, and if it is true that you have no true lawful and legiti-mate brothers—

MARIE-SIDONIE. No, M'su.

M. CAHUSAC. Then, Mamselle, I have nothing further to do than to announce to you that you are the true and long-lost heir to the throne of France.

> *He draws himself up, approaches her with great dignity, and kisses her hand.* Marie-Sidonie *begins to cry. He goes to the desk, pours out a glass of water and murmuring,* "Your Royal Highness," *offers it to her.*

MARIE-SIDONIE. M'su Cahusac, I am very sorry. . . . But there must be some mistake. My father was a poor sailor . . . a . . . a poor sailor.

M. CAHUSAC (*reading from his papers*). . . . A distinguished and esteemed navigator.

MARIE-SIDONIE. . . . A poor sailor . . .

M. CAHUSAC (*firmly*). . . . Navigator . . .

Pause. She looks about, stricken.

MARIE-SIDONIE (*as before, suddenly and loudly*). M'su, what danger am I in?

M. CAHUSAC (*approaching her and lowering his voice*). As Your Royal Highness knows there are several families in New Orleans that claim, without documents (*he rattles the vellum and seals in his hand*), without proof—that pretend to the blood royal. The danger from them, however, is not great. The real danger is from France. From the impassioned Republicans.

MARIE-SIDONIE. Impass . . .

M. CAHUSAC. But Your Royal Highness has only to put Herself into my hands.

MARIE-SIDONIE (*crying again*). Please do not call me "Your Royal Highness."

M. CAHUSAC. You . . . give me permission to call you Madame de Cressaux?

MARIE-SIDONIE. Yes, M'su. Mamselle Cressaux. I am Marie-Sidonie Cressaux.

M. CAHUSAC. Am I mistaken . . . hmm . . . in saying that you have children?

MARIE-SIDONIE (*faintly*). Yes, M'su. I have three children.

M. Cahusac *looks at her thoughtfully a moment and returns to his desk.*

M. CAHUSAC. Madame, from now on thousands of eyes will be fixed upon you, the eyes of the whole world, Madame. I cannot urge you too strongly to be very discreet, to be very circumspect.

MARIE-SIDONIE (*rising, abruptly, nervously*). M'su Cahusac, I do not wish to have anything to do with this. There is a mistake somewhere. I thank you very much, but there is a mistake somewhere. I do not know where. I must go now.

M. CAHUSAC (*darts forward*). But, Madame, you do not know what you are doing. Your rank cannot be dismissed as easily as that. Do you not know that in a month or two, all the newspapers in the world, including the New Orleans *Times-Picayune,* will publish your name? The first nobles of France will cross the ocean to call upon you. The Bishop of Louisiana will call upon you . . . the Mayor . . .

MARIE-SIDONIE. No, no.

M. CAHUSAC. You will be given a great deal of money—and several palaces.

MARIE-SIDONIE. No, no.

M. CAHUSAC. And a guard of soldiers to protect you.

MARIE-SIDONIE. No, no.

M. CAHUSAC. You will be made president of Le Petit Salon and Queen of the Mardi Gras. . . . Another sip of water, Your Royal Highness.

MARIE-SIDONIE. Oh, M'su, what shall I do?
. . . Oh, M'su, save me!—I do not want the
Bishop or the Mayor.

M. CAHUSAC. You ask me what you shall do?

MARIE-SIDONIE. Oh, yes, oh, my God!

M. CAHUSAC. For the present, return to your
home and lie down. A little rest and a little re-
flection will tell you what you have to do. Then
come and see me Thursday morning.

MARIE-SIDONIE. I think there must be a mistake somewhere.

M. CAHUSAC. May I be permitted to ask Madame de Cressaux a question: Could I have the
privilege of presenting Her—until the great announcement takes place—with a small gift of . . .
money?

MARIE-SIDONIE. No, no.

M. CAHUSAC. The Historical Society is not rich.
The Historical Society has difficulty in pursuing
the search for the last documents that will confirm
Madame's exalted rank, but they would be very
happy to advance a certain sum to Madame, sub-
scribed by her devoted subjects.

MARIE-SIDONIE. Please no. I do not wish any.
I must go now.

M. CAHUSAC. Let me beg Madame not to be
alarmed. For the present a little rest and reflec-
tion. . . .

> The bell rings. He again bends over her
> hand, murmuring . . . "obedient servant
> and devoted subject."

MARIE-SIDONIE (*in confusion*). Goodbye, good morning, M. Cahusac. (*She lingers at the door a moment, then returns and says in great earnestness*): Oh, M. Cahusac, do not let the Bishop come and see me. The Mayor, yes—but not the Bishop.

> *Enter* Madame Pugeot, *a plump little bourgeoise in black.*

> *Exit* Marie-Sidonie. M. Cahusac *kisses the graciously extended hand of* Madame Pugeot.

MME. PUGEOT. Good morning, M. Cahusac.

M. CAHUSAC. Your Royal Highness.

MME. PUGEOT. What business can you possibly be having with that dreadful Marie Cressaux! Do you not know that she is an abandoned woman?

M. CAHUSAC. Alas, we are in the world, Your Royal Highness. For the present I must earn a living as best I can. Mamselle Cressaux is arranging about the purchase of a house and garden.

MME. PUGEOT. Purchase, M. Cahusac, phi! You know very well that she has half a dozen houses and gardens already. She persuades every one of her lovers to give her a little house and garden. She is beginning to own the whole parish of Saint-Magloire.

M. CAHUSAC. Will Your Royal Highness condescend to sit down? (*She does.*) And how is the royal family this morning?

MME. PUGEOT. Only so-so, M'su Cahusac.

M. CAHUSAC. The Archduchess of Tuscany?

MME. PUGEOT (*fanning herself with a turkey's*

wing). A cold. One of her colds. I sometimes think
the dear child will never live to see her pearls.

M. CAHUSAC. And the Dauphin, Your Royal
Highness?

MME. PUGEOT. Still, still amusing himself in
the city, as young men will. Wine, gambling, bad
company. At least it keeps him out of harm.

M. CAHUSAC. And the Duke of Burgundy?

MME. PUGEOT. Imagine! The poor child has a
sty in his eye!

M. CAHUSAC. Tchk-tchk! (*with solicitude*) In
which eye, Madame?

MME. PUGEOT. In the left!

M. CAHUSAC. Tchk-tchk! And the Prince of
Lorraine and the Duke of Berry?

MME. PUGEOT. They are fairly well, but they
seem to mope in their cradle. Their first teeth, my
dear chamberlain.

M. CAHUSAC. And your husband, Madame?

MME. PUGEOT (*rises, walks back and forth a
moment, then stands still*). From now on we are
never to mention him again—while we are dis-
cussing these matters. It is to be understood that
he is my husband in a manner of speaking only.
He has no part in my true life. He has chosen to
scoff at my birth and my rank, but he will see
what he will see. . . . Naturally I have not told
him about the proofs that you and I have collected. I have not the heart to let him see how
unimportant he will become.

M. CAHUSAC. Unimportant, indeed!

MME. PUGEOT. So remember, we do not mention him in the same breath *with these matters!*

M. CAHUSAC. You must trust me, Madame. (*softly, with significance*) And *your* health, Your Royal Highness?

MME. PUGEOT. Oh, very well, thank you. Excellent. I used to do quite poorly, as you remember, but since this wonderful news I have been more than well, God be praised.

M. CAHUSAC (*as before, with lifted eyebrows*). I beg of you to do nothing unwise. I beg of you. . . . The little new life we are all anticipating . . .

MME. PUGEOT. Have no fear, my dear chamberlain. What is dear to France is dear to me.

M. CAHUSAC. When I think, Madame, of how soon we shall be able to announce your rank— when I think that this time next year you will be enjoying all the honors and privileges that are your due, I am filled with a pious joy.

MME. PUGEOT. God's will be done, God's will be done.

M. CAHUSAC. At all events, I am particularly happy to see that Your Royal Highness is in the best of health, for I have had a piece of disappointing news.

MME. PUGEOT. Chamberlain, you are not going to tell me that Germany has at last declared war upon my country?

M. CAHUSAC. No, Madame.

MME. PUGEOT. You greatly frightened me last

week. I could scarcely sleep. Such burdens as I have! My husband tells me that I cried out in my sleep the words: *Paris, I come!*

M. CAHUSAC. Sublime, Madame!

MME. PUGEOT. *Paris, I come,* like that. I cried out twice in my sleep: *Paris, I come.* Oh, these are anxious times; I am on my way to the Cathedral now. This Bismarck does not understand me. We must avoid a war at all costs, M. Cahusac. . . . Then what is your news?

M. CAHUSAC. My anxiety at present is more personal. The Historical Society in Paris is now confirming the last proofs of your claim. They have secretaries at work in all the archives: Madrid, Vienna, Constantinople . . .

MME. PUGEOT. Constantinople!

M. CAHUSAC. All this requires a good deal of money and the Society is not rich. We have been driven to a painful decision. The Society must sell one of the royal jewels or one of the royal *fournitures* which I am guarding upstairs. The Historical Society has written me, Madame, ordering me to send them at once—the royal christening robe.

MME. PUGEOT. Never!

M. CAHUSAC. The very robe under which Charlemagne was christened, the Charles, the Henris, the Louis, to lie under a glass in the Louvre. (*softly*) And this is particularly painful to me because I had hoped—it was, in fact, the dream of

my life—to see at least one of your children christened under all those fleurs-de-lis.

MME. PUGEOT. It shall not go to the Louvre.
I forbid it.

M. CAHUSAC. But what can I do? I offered them
the scepter. I offered them the orb. I even offered
them the mug which Your Royal Highness has
already purchased. But no! the christening robe
it must be.

MME. PUGEOT. It shall not leave America!
(*clutching her handbag*) How much are they asking for it?

M. CAHUSAC. Oh, Madame, since it is the Ministry of Museums and Monuments they are asking
a great many thousands of francs.

MME. PUGEOT. And how much would they ask
their Queen?

M. CAHUSAC (*sadly*). Madame, Madame, I cannot see you purchasing those things which are
rightly yours.

MME. PUGEOT. I will purchase it. I shall sell
the house on the Chausée Sainte Anne.

M. CAHUSAC (*softly*). If Your Majesty will give
five hundred dollars of Her money I shall add
five hundred of my own.

MME. PUGEOT (*shaken*). Five hundred. Five
hundred. . . . Well, you will be repaid many
times, my dear chamberlain, when I am restored
to my position. (*She thinks a moment.*) To-morrow at three, I shall bring you the papers for the

sale of the house. You will do everything quietly.
My husband will be told about it in due time.

M. CAHUSAC. I understand. I shall be very discreet.

> *The bell rings.* M. Cahusac *turns to the door
> as* Mamselle Pointevin *starts to enter.*

I shall be free to see you in a few moments,
Mamselle. Madame Pugeot has still some details
to discuss with me.

MLLE. POINTEVIN. I cannot wait long, M'su
Cahusac.

M. CAHUSAC. A few minutes in the Park, thank
you, Mamselle.

> *Exit* Mamselle Pointevin.

MME. PUGEOT. Has that poor girl business with
a lawyer, M. Cahusac? A poor school-teacher like
that?

M. CAHUSAC (*softly*). Mamselle Pointevin has
taken it into her head to make her will.

MME. PUGEOT (*laughs superiorly*). Three chairs
and a broken plate. (*rising*) Well, to-morrow at
three. . . . I am now going to the Cathedral. I
do not forget the great responsibilities for which
I must prepare myself—the army, the navy, the
treasury, the appointment of bishops. When I
am dead, my dear chamberlain—

M. CAHUSAC. Madame!

MME. PUGEOT. No, no!—even I must die some
day. . . . When I am dead, when I am laid with
my ancestors, let it never be said of me . . . By
the way, where shall I be laid?

M. Cahusac. In the church of St. Denis, Your Royal Highness?

Mme. Pugeot. Not in Notre-Dame?

M. Cahusac. No, Madame.

Mme. Pugeot (*meditatively*). Not in Notre-Dame. Well (*brightening*) we will cross these bridges when we get to them. (*extending her hand*) Good morning and all my thanks, my dear chamberlain.

M. Cahusac. . . . Highness' most obedient servant and devoted subject.

Mme. Pugeot (*beautifully, filling the doorway*). Pray for us.

> *Exit* Madame Pugeot. M. Cahusac *goes to the door and bows to* Mamselle Pointevin *in the street.*

M. Cahusac. Now Mamselle, if you will have the goodness to enter.

> *Enter* Mamselle Pointevin, *a tall and indignant spinster.*

Mlle. Pointevin. M'su Cahusac, it is something new for you to keep me waiting in the public square while you carry on your wretched little business with a vulgar woman like Madame Pugeot. When I condescend to call upon you, my good man, you will have the goodness to receive me at once. Either I am, or I am not, Henriette, Queen of France, Queen of Navarre and Aquitania. It is not fitting that we cool our heels on a public bench among the nursemaids of remote New Orleans. It is hard enough for me to *hide myself* as a schoolmistress in this city, without having to suffer further humiliations at your hands. Is there no respect due to the blood of Charlemagne?

M. CAHUSAC. Madame . . .

MLLE. POINTEVIN. Or, Sir, are you bored and overfed on the company of queens?

M. CAHUSAC. Madame . . .

MLLE. POINTEVIN. You are busy with the law. Good! Know, then, *La loi—c'est moi. (sitting down and smoothing out her skirts)* Now what is it you have to say?

M. CAHUSAC *(pauses a moment, then approaches her with tightly pressed lips and narrowed eyes)*. Your Royal Highness, I have received a letter from France. There is some discouraging news.

MLLE. POINTEVIN. No! I cannot afford to buy another thing. I possess the scepter and the orb. Sell the rest to the Louvre, if you must. I can buy them back when my rank is announced.

M. CAHUSAC. Alas!

MLLE. POINTEVIN. What do you mean—"alas"?

M. CAHUSAC. Will Your Royal Highness condescend to read the letter I have received from France?

MLLE. POINTEVIN *(unfurls the letter, but continues looking before her, splendidly)*. Have they no bread? Give them cake. *(She starts to read, is shaken, suddenly returns it to him.)* It is too long. It is too long. . . . What does it say?

M. CAHUSAC. It is from the Secretary of the Historical Society. The Society remains convinced that you are the true and long-sought heir to the throne of France.

MLLE. POINTEVIN. Convinced? Convinced? I should hope so.

M. CAHUSAC. But to make this conviction public, Madame, to announce it throughout the newspapers of the world, including the New Orleans *Times-Picayune* . . .

MLLE. POINTEVIN. Yes, go on!

M. CAHUSAC. To establish your claim among all your rivals. To establish your claim beyond any possible ridicule . . .

MLLE. POINTEVIN. Ridicule!

M. CAHUSAC. All they lack is one little document. One little but important document. They had hoped to find it in the archives of Madrid. Madame, it is not there.

MLLE. POINTEVIN. It is not there? Then where is it?

M. CAHUSAC. We do not know, Your Royal Highness. We are in despair.

MLLE. POINTEVIN. Ridicule, M. Cahusac!

She stares at him, her hand on her mouth.

M. CAHUSAC. It may be in Constantinople. It may be in Vienna. Naturally we shall continue to search for it. We shall continue to search for generations, for centuries, if need be. But I must confess this is a very discouraging blow.

MLLE. POINTEVIN. Generations! Centuries! But

I am not a young girl, M'su Cahusac. Their letter says over and over again that I am the heir to the throne. (*She begins to cry.*)

M. Cahusac *discreetly proffers her a glass of water.*

MLLE. POINTEVIN. Thank you.

M. CAHUSAC (*suddenly changing his tone, with firmness*). Madame, you should know that the Society suspects the lost document to be in your possession. The Society feels sure that the document has been handed down from generation to generation in your family.

MLLE. POINTEVIN. In my possession!

M. CAHUSAC (*firmly*). Madame, are you concealing something from us?

MLLE. POINTEVIN. Why . . . no.

M. CAHUSAC. Are you playing with us, as a cat plays with a mouse?

MLLE. POINTEVIN. No, indeed I'm not.

M. CAHUSAC. Why is that paper not in Madrid, or in Constantinople or in Vienna? *Because it is in your house.* You live in what was once your father's house, do you not?

MLLE. POINTEVIN. Yes, I do.

M. CAHUSAC. Go back to it. Look through every old trunk . . .

MLLE. POINTEVIN. Every old trunk!

M. CAHUSAC. Examine especially the linings. Look through all the tables and desks. Pry into the joints. You will find perhaps a secret drawer, a secret panel.

MLLE. POINTEVIN. M'su Cahusac!

M. CAHUSAC. Examine the walls. Examine the boards of the floor. It may be hidden beneath them.

MLLE. POINTEVIN. I will. I'll go now.

M. CAHUSAC. Have you any old clothes of your father?

MLLE. POINTEVIN. Yes, I have.

M. CAHUSAC. It may be sewn into the lining.

MLLE. POINTEVIN. I'll look.

M. CAHUSAC. Madame, in what suit of clothes was your father buried?

MLLE. POINTEVIN. In his best, M'su.

She gives a sudden scream under her hand as this thought strikes home. They stare at one another significantly.

M. CAHUSAC. Take particular pains to look under all steps. These kinds of document are frequently found under steps. You will find it. If it is not in Madrid, it is there.

MLLE. POINTEVIN. But if I can't find it! (*She sits down, suddenly spent.*) No one will ever know that I am the Queen of France. (*pause*) I am very much afraid, M'su Cahusac, that I shall never find that document in my four rooms. I know every inch of them. But I shall look. (*She draws her hand across her forehead, as though awaking from a dream.*) It is all very strange. You know, M'su Cahusac, I think there may have been a mistake somewhere. It was so beautiful while it lasted. It made even school-teaching a pleasure, M'su. . . . And my memoirs. I have just written my memoirs up to the moment when your wonderful announcement came to me—the account of my childhood *incognito,* the little girl in Louisiana who did not guess the great things before her. But before I go, may I ask something of you? Will you have the Historical Society write me a letter saying that they seriously think I may be . . . the person . . . the person they are looking for? I wish to keep the letter in the trunk with the orb and . . . with the scepter. You know . . . the more I think of it, the more I think there must have been a mistake somewhere.

M. CAHUSAC. The very letter you have in mind is here, Madame.

He gives it to her.

MLLE. POINTEVIN. Thank you. And M'su Cahusac, may I ask another favor of you?

M. CAHUSAC. Certainly, Madame.

MLLE. POINTEVIN. Please, never mention this . . . this whole affair to anyone in New Orleans.

M. CAHUSAC. Madame, not unless you wish it.

MLLE. POINTEVIN. Good morning—good morning, and thank you.

Her handkerchief to one eye she goes out.

M. Cahusac *goes to his desk.*

The bell rings.

The reed curtain is parted and a Negro boy pushes in a wheel chair containing a woman of some hundred years of age. She is wrapped in shawls, like a mummy, and wears a scarf about her head, and green spectacles on her nose. The mummy extends a hand which M. Cahusac *kisses devotedly, murmuring,* "Your Royal Highness."

The curtain falls.

Pullman Car Hiawatha

*At the back of the stage is a balcony or bridge or
runway leading out of sight in both directions.
Two flights of stairs descend from it to the
stage. There is no further scenery.*
At the rise of the curtain the Stage Manager *is
making lines with a piece of chalk on the floor
of the stage by the footlights.*

THE STAGE MANAGER. This is the plan of a
Pullman car. Its name is Hiawatha and on December twenty-first it is on its way from New York
to Chicago. Here at your left are three compartments. Here is the aisle and five lowers. The
berths are all full, uppers and lowers, but for the
purposes of this play we are limiting our interest
to the people in the lower berths on the further
side only.

The berths are already made up. It is half-past
nine. Most of the passengers are in bed behind
the green curtains. They are dropping their shoes
on the floor, or wrestling with their trousers, or
wondering whether they dare hide their valuables
in the pillow-slips during the night.

All right! Come on, everybody!
*The actors enter carrying chairs. Each improvises
his berth by placing two chairs "facing one another" in his chalk-marked space. They then
sit in one chair, profile to the audience, and rest*

*their feet on the other. This must do for lying
in bed.*

*The passengers in the compartments do the same.
Reading from left to right we have:*

Compartment Three: *An insane woman with a
male attendant and a trained nurse.*

Compartment Two: Philip *and*

Compartment One: Harriet, *his young wife.*

Lower One: *A maiden lady.*

Lower Three: *A middle-aged doctor.*

Lower Five: *A stout, amiable woman of fifty.*

Lower Seven: *An engineer going to California.*

Lower Nine: *Another engineer.*

LOWER ONE. Porter, be sure and wake me up at
quarter of six.

PORTER. Yes, mam.

LOWER ONE. I know I shan't sleep a wink, but
I want to be told when it's quarter of six.

PORTER. Yes, mam.

LOWER SEVEN (*putting his head through the
curtains*). Hsst! Porter! Hsst! How the hell do you
turn on this other light?

PORTER (*fussing with it*). I'm afraid it's outa
order, suh. You'll have to use the other end.

THE STAGE MANAGER (*falsetto, substituting for
some woman in an upper berth*). May I ask if
some one in this car will be kind enough to lend
me some aspirin?

PORTER. (*rushing about*). Yes, mam.

LOWER NINE (*one of these engineers, descend-*

ing the aisle and falling into Lower Five). Sorry, lady, sorry. Made a mistake.

LOWER FIVE (*grumbling*). Never in all my born days!

LOWER ONE (*in a shrill whisper*). Porter! Porter!

PORTER. Yes, mam.

LOWER ONE. My hot water bag's leaking. I guess you'll have to take it away. I'll have to do without it tonight. How awful!

LOWER FIVE (*sharply to the passenger above her*). Young man, you mind your own business, or I'll report you to the conductor.

STAGE MANAGER (*substituting for* Upper Five). Sorry, mam, I didn't mean to upset you. My suspenders fell down and I was trying to catch them.

LOWER FIVE. Well, here they are. Now go to sleep. Everybody seems to be rushing into my berth tonight.

She puts her head out.

Porter! Porter! Be a good soul and bring me a glass of water, will you? I'm parched.

LOWER NINE. Bill!

No answer.

Bill!

LOWER SEVEN. Ye'? Wha' d'y'a want?

LOWER NINE. Slip me one of those magazines, willya?

LOWER SEVEN. Which one d'y'a want?

LOWER NINE. Either one. "Detective Stories." Either one.

LOWER SEVEN. Aw, Fred. I'm just in the middle of one of'm in "Detective Stories."

LOWER NINE. That's all right. I'll take the "Western."—Thanks.

THE STAGE MANAGER (*to the actors*). All right! —Sh! Sh! Sh!—.

To the audience.

Now I want you to hear them thinking.

There is a pause and then they all begin a murmuring-swishing noise, very soft. In turn each one of them can be heard above the others.

LOWER FIVE (*the lady of fifty*). Let's see: I've got the doll for the baby. And the slip-on for Marietta. And the fountain pen for Herbert. And the subscription to *Time* for George. . . .

LOWER SEVEN (*Bill*). God! Lillian, if you don't turn out to be what I think you are, I don't know what I'll do.—I guess it's bad politics to let a woman know that you're going all the way to California to see her. I'll think up a song-and-dance about a business trip or something. Was I ever as hot and bothered about anyone like this before? Well, there was Martha. But that was different. I'd better try and read or I'll go cookoo. "How did you know it was ten o'clock when the visitor left the house?" asked the detective. "Because at ten o'clock," answered the girl, "I always turn out the lights in the conservatory and in the back hall. As I was coming down the stairs I heard the master talking to someone at the front door. I heard him say, 'Well, good night . . .' "—Gee, I don't feel like reading; I'll just think about Lillian. That yellow hair. Them eyes! . . .

LOWER THREE (*the doctor reads aloud to himself from a medical journal the most hair-raising material, every now and then punctuating his reading with an interrogative "So?"*).

LOWER ONE (*the maiden lady*). I know I'll be awake all night. I might just as well make up my mind to it now. I can't imagine what got hold of that hot water bag to leak on the train of all places. Well now, I'll lie on my right side and breathe deeply and think of beautiful things, and perhaps I can doze off a bit.

and lastly:

LOWER NINE (*Fred*). That was the craziest thing I ever did. It's set me back three whole years. I could have saved up thirty thousand dollars by now, if I'd only stayed over here. What business had I got to fool with contracts with the goddam Soviets. Hell, I thought it would be interesting. Interesting, what-the-hell! It's set me back three whole years. I don't even know if the company'll take me back. I'm green, that's all. I just don't grow up.

The Stage Manager *strides toward them with lifted hand crying "Hush," and their whispering ceases.*

THE STAGE MANAGER. That'll do!—Just one minute. Porter!

THE PORTER (*appearing at the left*). Yessuh.

THE STAGE MANAGER. It's your turn to think.

THE PORTER (*is very embarrassed*).

THE STAGE MANAGER. Don't you want to? You have a right to.

THE PORTER (*torn between the desire to release his thoughts and his shyness*). Ah . . . ah . . . I'm only thinkin' about my home in Chicago and . . . and my life insurance.

THE STAGE MANAGER. That's right.

THE PORTER. . . . well, thank you. . . . Thank you.

> *He slips away, blushing violently, in an agony of self-consciousness and pleasure.*

THE STAGE MANAGER (*to the audience*). He's a good fellow, Harrison is. Just shy.

> *To the actors again.*

Now the compartments, please.

> *The berths fall into shadow.*
>
> Philip *is standing at the door connecting his compartment with his wife's.*

PHILIP. Are you all right, angel?

HARRIET. Yes. I don't know what was the matter with me during dinner.

PHILIP. Shall I close the door?

HARRIET. Do see whether you can't put a chair against it that will hold it half open without banging.

PHILIP. There.—Good night, angel. If you can't sleep, call me and we'll sit up and play Russian Bank.

HARRIET. You're thinking of that awful time

when we sat up every night for a week. . . . But at least I know I shall sleep tonight. The noise of the wheels has become sort of nice and homely. What state are we in?

PHILIP. We're tearing through Ohio. We'll be in Indiana soon.

HARRIET. I know those little towns full of horse-blocks.

PHILIP. Well, we'll reach Chicago very early. I'll call you. Sleep tight.

HARRIET. Sleep tight, darling.

> *He returns to his own compartment. In Compartment Three, the male attendant tips his chair back against the wall and smokes a cigar. The trained nurse knits a stocking. The insane woman leans her forehead against the windowpane, that is: stares into the audience.*

THE INSANE WOMAN (*her words have a dragging, complaining sound, but lack any conviction*). Don't take me there. Don't take me there.

THE FEMALE ATTENDANT. Wouldn't you like to lie down, dearie?

THE INSANE WOMAN. I want to get off the train. I want to go back to New York.

THE FEMALE ATTENDANT. Wouldn't you like me to brush your hair again? It's such a nice feeling.

THE INSANE WOMAN (*going to the door*). I want to get off the train. I want to open the door.

THE FEMALE ATTENDANT (*taking one of her*

hands). Such a noise! You'll wake up all the nice people. Come and I'll tell you a story about the place we're going to.

THE INSANE WOMAN. I don't want to go to that place.

THE FEMALE ATTENDANT. Oh, it's lovely! There are lawns and gardens everywhere. I never saw such a lovely place. Just lovely.

THE INSANE WOMAN (*lies down on the bed*). Are there roses?

THE FEMALE ATTENDANT. Roses! Red, yellow, white . . . just everywhere.

THE MALE ATTENDANT (*after a pause*). That musta been Cleveland.

THE FEMALE ATTENDANT. I had a case in Cleveland once. Diabetes.

THE MALE ATTENDANT (*after another pause*). I wisht I had a radio here. Radios are good for *them*. I had a patient once that had to have the radio going every minute.

THE FEMALE ATTENDANT. Radios are lovely. My married niece has one. It's always going. It's wonderful.

THE INSANE WOMAN (*half rising*). I'm not beautiful. I'm not beautiful as she was.

THE FEMALE ATTENDANT. Oh, I think you're beautiful! Beautiful.—Mr. Morgan, don't you think Mrs. Churchill is beautiful?

THE MALE ATTENDANT. Oh, fine lookin'! Regular movie star, Mrs. Churchill.

She looks inquiringly at them and subsides.

Harriet *groans slightly. Smothers a cough.*
She gropes about with her hand and finds the
bell.

The Porter *knocks at her door.*

HARRIET (*whispering*). Come in. First, please
close the door into my husband's room. Softly.
Softly.

PORTER (*a plaintive porter*). Yes, mam.

HARRIET. Porter, I'm not well. I'm sick. I must
see a doctor.

PORTER. Why, mam, they ain't no doctor . . .

HARRIET. Yes, when I was coming out from
dinner I saw a man in one of the seats on *that*
side, reading medical papers. Go and wake him
up.

PORTER (*flabbergasted*). Mam, I cain't wake
anybody up.

HARRIET. Yes, you can. Porter. Porter. Now
don't argue with me. I'm very sick. It's my heart.
Wake him up. Tell him it's my heart.

PORTER. Yes, mam.

He goes into the aisle and starts pulling the
shoulder of the man in Lower Three.

LOWER THREE. Hello. Hello. What is it? Are
we there?

The Porter *mumbles to him.*

I'll be right there.—Porter, is it a young woman
or an old one?

PORTER. I dono, suh. I guess she's kinda old,
suh, but not so very old.

LOWER THREE. Tell her I'll be there in a minute and to lie quietly.

The Porter *enters* Harriet's *compartment. She has turned her head away.*

PORTER. He'll be here in a minute, mam. He says you lie quiet.

Lower Three *stumbles along the aisle muttering:* "Damn these shoes!"

SOMEONE'S VOICE. Can't we have a little quiet in this car, please?

LOWER NINE (*Fred*). Oh, shut up!

The Doctor *passes the* Porter *and enters* Harriet's *compartment. He leans over her, concealing her by his stooping figure.*

LOWER THREE. She's dead, porter. Is there anyone on the train traveling with her?

PORTER. Yessuh. Dat's her husband in dere.

LOWER THREE. Idiot! Why didn't you call him? I'll go in and speak to him.

The Stage Manager *comes forward.*

THE STAGE MANAGER. All right. So much for the inside of the car. That'll be enough of that for the present. Now for its position geographically, meteorologically, astronomically, theologically considered.

Pullman Car Hiawatha, ten minutes of ten. December twenty-first, 1930. All ready.

Some figures begin to appear on the balcony. No, no. It's not time for the planets yet. Nor the hours.

They retire.

The Stage Manager *claps his hands. A grin-
ning boy in overalls enters from the left behind the berths.*

GROVER'S CORNERS, OHIO (*in a foolish voice as
though he were reciting a piece at a Sunday School
entertainment*). I represent Grover's Corners,
Ohio. 821 souls. "There's so much good in the
worst of us and so much bad in the best of us,
that it ill behooves any of us to criticize the rest
of us." Robert Louis Stevenson. Thankya.

He grins and goes out right.
*Enter from the same direction somebody in
shirt sleeves. This is a field.*

THE FIELD. I represent a field you are passing
between Grover's Corners, Ohio, and Parkersburg, Ohio. In this field there are 51 gophers, 206
field mice, 6 snakes and millions of bugs, insects,
ants, and spiders. All in their winter sleep. "What
is so rare as a day in June? Then, if ever, come
perfect days." *The Vision of Sir Launfal,* William
Cullen—I mean James Russell Lowell. Thank
you.

Exit.
Enter a tramp.

THE TRAMP. I just want to tell you that I'm a
tramp that's been traveling under this car, Hiawatha, so I have a right to be in this play. I'm going
from Rochester, New York, to Joliet, Illinois. It
takes a lotta people to make a world. "On the
road to Mandalay, where the flying fishes play and
the sun comes up like thunder, over China cross

the bay." Frank W. Service. It's bitter cold. Thank
you.

Exit.

*Enter a gentle old farmer's wife with three
stringy young people.*

PARKERSBURG, OHIO. I represent Parkersburg,
Ohio. 2604 souls. I have seen all the dreadful
havoc that alcohol has done and I hope no one
here will ever touch a drop of the curse of this
beautiful country.

*She beats a measure and they all sing un-
steadily:*

"Throw out the lifeline! Throw out the lifeline!
Someone is sinking today-ay . . ."

The Stage Manager *waves them away tact-
fully.*

Enter a workman.

THE WORKMAN. Ich bin der Arbeiter der hier
sein Leben verlor. Bei der Sprengung für diese
Brücke über die Sie in dem Moment fahren—

The engine whistles for a trestle crossing—
erschlug mich ein Felsbock. Ich spiele jetzt als
Geist in diesem Stuck mit. "Vor sieben und
achtzig Jahren haben unsere Väter auf diesem
Continent eine neue Nation hervorgebracht.
. . ."

THE STAGE MANAGER (*helpfully, to the audience*). I'm sorry; that's in German. He says that
he's the ghost of a workman who was killed while
they were building the trestle over which the
car Hiawatha is now passing—

The engine whistles again—
and he wants to appear in this play. A chunk of
rock hit him while they were dynamiting.—His
motto you know: "Three score and seven years
ago our fathers brought forth upon this continent
a new nation dedicated," and so on. Thank you,
Mr. Krüger.

Exit the ghost.

Enter another worker.

THIS WORKER. I'm a watchman in a tower near
Parkersburg, Ohio. I just want to tell you that
I'm not asleep and that the signals are all right
for this train. I hope you all have a fine trip. "If
you can keep your heads when all about you are
losing theirs and blaming it on you. . . ." Rud-
yard Kipling. Thank you.

Exit.

The Stage Manager *comes forward.*

THE STAGE MANAGER. All right. That'll be
enough of that. Now the weather.

Enter a mechanic.

A MECHANIC. It is eleven degrees above zero.
The wind is north-northwest, velocity, 57. There
is a field of low barometric pressure moving east-
ward from Saskatchewan to the Eastern Coast.
Tomorrow it will be cold with some snow in the
Middle Western States and Northern New York.

Exit.

THE STAGE MANAGER. All right. Now for the
hours.

Helpfully to the audience:

The minutes are gossips; the hours are philosophers; the years are theologians. The hours are philosophers with the exception of Twelve O'clock who is also a theologian.—Ready Ten O'clock!

> *The hours are beautiful girls dressed like Elihu Vedder's Pleiades. Each carries a great gold Roman numeral. They pass slowly across the balcony at the back moving from right to left.*

What are you doing, Ten O'clock? Aristotle?

TEN O'CLOCK. No, Plato, Mr. Washburn.

THE STAGE MANAGER. Good.—"Are you not rather convinced that he who thus . . ."

TEN O'CLOCK. "Are you not rather convinced that he who sees Beauty as only it can be seen will be specially favored? And since he is in contact not with images but with realities. . . ."

> *She continues the passage in a murmur as* Eleven O'clock *appears.*

ELEVEN O'CLOCK. "What else can I, Epictetus, do, a lame old man, but sing hymns to God? If then I were a nightingale, I would do the nightingale's part. If I were a swan I would do a swan's. But now I am a rational creature. . . ."

> *Her voice too subsides to a murmur.* Twelve O'clock *appears.*

THE STAGE MANAGER. Good.—Twelve O'clock, what have you?

TWELVE O'CLOCK. Saint Augustine and his mother.

THE STAGE MANAGER. So.—"And we began to say: If to any the tumult of the flesh were hushed. . . ."

TWELVE O'CLOCK. "And we began to say: If to any the tumult of the flesh were hushed; hushed the images of earth; of waters and of air; . . .

THE STAGE MANAGER. Faster.—"Hushed also the poles of Heaven."

TWELVE O'CLOCK. "Yea, were the very soul to be hushed to herself."

STAGE MANAGER. A little louder, Miss Foster.

TWELVE O'CLOCK (*a little louder*). "Hushed all dreams and imaginary revelations. . . ."

THE STAGE MANAGER (*waving them back*). All right. All right. Now the planets. December twenty-first, 1930, please.

The hours unwind and return to their dressing rooms at the right. The planets appear on the balcony. Some of them take their place halfway on the steps. These have no words, but each has a sound. One has a pulsating, zinging sound. Another has a thrum. One whistles ascending and descending scales. Saturn does a slow, obstinate:

M—M—M—M—

Louder, Saturn.—Venus, higher. Good. Now, Jupiter.—Now the earth.

He turns to the beds on the train.

Come, everybody. This is the earth's sound.

The towns, workmen, etc. appear at the edge of the stage. The passengers begin their "thinking" murmur.

Come, Grover's Corners. Parkersburg. You're in this.

Watchman. Tramp. This is the earth's sound.

He conducts it as the director of an orchestra would. Each of the towns and workmen does his motto.

The Insane Woman *breaks into passionate weeping. She rises and stretches out her arms to the* Stage Manager.

THE INSANE WOMAN. Use me. Give me something to do.

He goes to her quickly, whispers something in her ear, and leads her back to her guardians. She is unconsoled.

THE STAGE MANAGER. Now sh—sh—sh! Enter the archangels.

To the audience:

THE STAGE MANAGER. We have now reached the theological position of Pullman Car Hiawatha.

The towns and workmen have disappeared. The planets, off stage, continue a faint music. Two young men in blue serge suits enter along the balcony and descend the stairs at the right. As they pass each bed the passenger talks in his sleep.

Gabriel *points out* Bill *to* Michael *who smiles with raised eyebrows. They pause before* Lower Five *and* Michael *makes the sound of assent that can only be rendered "Hn-Hn." The remarks that the characters make in their sleep are not all intelligible, being lost in the sound of sigh or groan or whisper by which they are conveyed. But we seem to hear:*

LOWER NINE (*loud*). Some people are slower than others, that's all.

LOWER SEVEN (*Bill*). It's no fun, y'know. I'll try.

LOWER FIVE (*the lady of the Christmas presents, rapidly*). You know best, of course. I'm ready whenever you are. One year's like another.

LOWER ONE. I can teach sewing. I can sew.

They approach Harriet's *compartment.*

The Insane Woman *sits up and speaks to them.*

THE INSANE WOMAN. Me?

THE ARCHANGELS (*shake their heads*).

THE INSANE WOMAN. What possible use can there be in my simply waiting?—Well, I'm grateful for anything. I'm grateful for being so much better than I was. The old story, the terrible story, doesn't haunt me as it used to. A great load seems to have been taken off my mind.—But no one understands me any more. At last I understand myself perfectly, but no one else understands a thing I say.—So I must wait?

THE ARCHANGELS (*nod, smiling*).

THE INSANE WOMAN (*resignedly, and with a smile that implies their complicity*). Well, you know best. I'll do whatever is best; but everyone is so childish, so absurd. They have no logic. These people are all so mad. . . . These people are like children; they have never suffered.

She returns to her bed and sleeps. The arch-angels *stand beside* Harriet. *The* doctor *has drawn* Philip *into the next compartment and is talking to him in earnest whispers.*

Harriet's *face has been toward the wall; she turns it slightly and speaks toward the ceiling.*

HARRIET. I wouldn't be happy there. Let me stay dead down here. I belong here. I shall be perfectly happy to roam about my house and be near Philip.—You know I wouldn't be happy there.

Gabriel *leans over and whispers into her ear. After a short pause she bursts into fierce tears.*

I'm ashamed to come with you. I haven't done anything. I haven't done anything with my life. Worse than that: I was angry and sullen. I never realized anything. I don't dare go a step in such a place.

They whisper to her again.

But it's not possible to forgive such things. I don't want to be forgiven so easily. I want to be punished for it all. I won't stir until I've been

punished a long, long time. I want to be freed of
all that—by punishment. I want to be all new.

*They whisper to her. She puts her feet slowly
on the ground.*

But no one else could be punished for me. I'm
willing to face it all myself. I don't ask anyone to
be punished for me.

*They whisper to her again. She sits long and
brokenly looking at her shoes and thinking
it over.*

It wasn't fair. I'd have been willing to suffer for
it myself,—if I could have endured such a moun-
tain.

She smiles.

Oh, I'm ashamed! I'm just a stupid and you
know it. I'm just another American.—But then
what wonderful things must be beginning now.
You really want me? You really want me?

*They start leading her down the aisle of the
car.*

Let's take the whole train. There are some
lovely faces on this train. Can't we all come? You'll
never find anyone better than Philip. Please,
please, let's all go.

They reach the steps. The archangels *inter-
lock their arms as a support for her as she
leans heavily on them, taking the steps slowly.
Her words are half singing and half bab-
bling.*

But look at how tremendously high and far it
is. I've a weak heart. I'm not supposed to climb

stairs. "I do not ask to see the distant scene: One step enough for me." It's like Switzerland. My tongue keeps saying things. I can't control it.— Do let me stop a minute: I want to say goodbye.

She turns in their arms.

Just a minute, I want to cry on your shoulder. *She leans her forehead against Gabriel's shoulder and laughs long and softly.*

Goodbye, Philip.—I begged him not to marry me, but he would. He believed in me just as you do.—Goodbye, 1312 Ridgewood Avenue, Oaksbury, Illinois. I hope I remember all its steps and doors and wallpapers forever. Goodbye, Emerson Grammar School on the corner of Forbush Avenue and Wherry Street. Goodbye, Miss Walker and Miss Cramer who taught me English and Miss Matthewson who taught me Biology. Goodbye, First Congregational Church on the corner of Meyerson Avenue and 6th Street and Dr. McReady and Mrs. McReady and Julia. Goodbye, Papa and Mama. . . .

She turns.

Now I'm tired of saying goodbye.—I never used to talk like this. I was so homely I never used to have the courage to talk. Until Philip came. I see now. I see now. I understand everything now.

The Stage Manager *comes forward.*

THE STAGE MANAGER (*to the actors*). All right. All right.—Now we'll have the whole world together, please. The whole solar system, please.

The complete cast begins to appear at the edges of the stage. He claps his hands.

The whole solar system, please. Where's the tramp?—Where's the moon?

He gives two raps on the floor, like the conductor of an orchestra attracting the attention of his forces, and slowly lifts his hand. The human beings murmur their thoughts; The hours discourse; the planets chant or hum. Harriet's *voice finally rises above them all saying:*

HARRIET. "I was not ever thus, nor asked that Thou
Shouldst lead me on, and spite of fears,
Pride ruled my will: Remember not past years."

The Stage Manager *waves them away.*

THE STAGE MANAGER. Very good. Now clear the stage, please. Now we're at Englewood Station, South Chicago. See the University's towers over there! The best of them all.

LOWER ONE (*the spinster*). Porter, you promised to wake me up at quarter of six.

PORTER. Sorry, mam, but it's been an awful night on this car. A lady's been terrible sick.

LOWER ONE. Oh! Is she better?

PORTER. No'm. She ain't one jot better.

LOWER FIVE. Young man, take your foot out of my face.

THE STAGE MANAGER (*again substituting for* Upper Five). Sorry, lady, I slipped—

LOWER FIVE (*grumbling not unamiably*). I declare, this trip's been one long series of insults.

THE STAGE MANAGER. Just one minute, mam, and I'll be down and out of your way.

LOWER FIVE. Haven't you got anybody to darn your socks for you? You ought to be ashamed to go about that way.

THE STAGE MANAGER. Sorry, lady.

LOWER FIVE. You're too stuck up to get married. That's the trouble with you.

LOWER NINE. Bill!—Bill!

LOWER SEVEN. Ye'? Wha' d'y'a want?

LOWER NINE. Bill, how much d'y'a give the porter on a train like this? I've been outa the country so long . . .

LOWER SEVEN. Hell, Fred, I don't know myself.

THE PORTER. CHICAGO, CHICAGO. All out. This train don't go no further.

The passengers jostle their way out and an army of old women with mops and pails enter and prepare to clean up the car.

The curtain falls.

Love and How To Cure It

The stage of the Tivoli Palace of Music, Soho, London, April, 1895.

The stage is dark save for a gas jet forward left and an oil lamp on the table at the back right.

Bare, dark, dusty and cold.

Linda, *dressed in a white ballet dress, is practicing steps and bending exercises. She is a beautiful, impersonal, remote, almost sullen girl of barely sixteen.*

At the table in the distance sit Joey, *a stout comedian, and* Rowena, *a mature soubrette.* Joey *is reading aloud from a pink theatrical and sporting weekly and* Rowena *is darning a stocking. When they speak the touch of cockney in their diction is insufficiently compensated by touches of exaggerated elegance.*

There is silence for a time, broken only by the undertone of the reading and the whispered counting of Linda *at her practice. Then:*

Rowena (*calling to* Linda). They've put off the rehearsal. Mark my words. It's after half-past eight now. They must have got word to the others somehow. Or else we understood the day wrong. —Go on, Joey.

He reads for a few minutes, then Rowena *calls again:*

Linda, the paper says Marjorie FitzMaurice has

an engagement. An Ali Baba and the Forty Thieves company that Moss has collected for Folkstone, Brighton, and the piers. She must have got better.—You'd better take a rest, dearie. You'll be all blowed.—Go on, Joey, that's a good boy.

LINDA (*gravely describing an arc waist-high with her toe*). It's nine o'clock. I can hear the chimes.

> *Apparently* Joey *has finished the paper. He stretches and yawns.* Rowena *puts down her work, picks up her chair and brings it toward the footlights, and starts firmly supervising* Linda's *movements.*

ROWENA. One, two, three; one, two, three. Whatever are you doing with your hands, child? Madame Angellelli didn't teach you anything like that. Bend them back like you was discovering a flower by surprise. That's right.—Upsidaisy! That's the way.—Now that's enough kicks for one night. If you must do any more, just stick to the knee-highs.

> *She yawns and pats her yawn.*

There's no rehearsal. We might just as well go home. It was all a mistake somehow.

LINDA (*almost upside down*). No, no. I don't want to go home. Besides, I'm hungry. Ask Joey to go around the corner and buy some fish and chips.

ROWENA. Goodness, I never saw such an eater. Well, I have two kippers here I was going to set on for breakfast.

Calling.

Joey, there's a stove downstairs still, isn't there?

Joey. Yes.

Rowena (*to Linda*). There you are! We could have a little supper and ask Joey. I have a packet of tea in my bag. How would you like that, angel?

Linda. Lovely.

Rowena. Joey, how would you like a little supper on the stage with kipper and tea and everything nice?

Joey. Like it! I'm that starved I could eat bones and all. Wot's more, I'll cook it for you. I'm the best·little cooker of a kipper for a copper you could 'ope to see.

Rowena (*meditatively*). You could use that in a song someday, Joey.—Shall I let him cook it, Linda?

Linda. Yes, let him cook it.

Joey. I'll just go next door and get a spoonful of butter.

Rowena. There's sixpence. Get some milk for the tea, too. Put some water on as you go out and I'll be down in a minute to make the tea.

Joey. Won't be a minute, my dears.

He hurries out.

There is a pause. Linda *stops her exercise and examines attentively each of the soles of her slippers in turn.*

Rowena. Joey must have cooked thousands of kippers in his day. All those last years when his wife was ill, he cooked everything for her. Good old Joey! He's all lost without her. And he wants me to talk about her all the time, only he doesn't want to bring her into the conversation first. You know, Henrietta du Vaux was wonderful, but I can't talk about her forever.

Another pause.

Linda, whatever are you thinking about all the time?

LINDA. Nothing.

ROWENA. Don't you say "Nothing." Come now, tell your Auntie. What is it you keep turning over in your mind all the time?

LINDA (*indifferently*). Well, almost nothing,— except that I'm going to be shot any minute.

ROWENA. Don't say such things, dearie. No one's going to shoot you. You ought to be ashamed to say such things.

LINDA (*pointing scornfully to the door*). He's out waiting in the street this very minute.

ROWENA. Why, he went back to his university didn't he? He's a student. They don't let them come to London whenever they want.

LINDA. Oh, I don't care! Let him shoot me. I wish I'd never seen him. What was he doing, any-way,—worming his way into Madame Angellelli's swarrays. He'd oughta stayed among his own people.

ROWENA. I'm going out into the street this minute to see if he's there. I can get the police after him for hounding a poor girl so. What's his name?

LINDA. Arthur Warburton. I tell you I don't care if he shoots me.

ROWENA (*sharply*). Now I won't have you saying things like that! Now mind! If he's out there Joey'll go and get him and we'll have a talk. When did you see him last?

LINDA. Sunday. We had tea at Richmond and went boating on the river.

ROWENA. Did you let him kiss you?

LINDA. I let him kiss me once when we floated under some willow trees. And then he kept talking so hot-headed that I didn't let him kiss me again, and I liked him less and less. All the way back on the bus, I didn't pay any attention to him; just looked into the street and said yes and no; and then I told him I was too busy to see him this week. I don't want to see him again.—Aunt Rowena, he breathes so hard.

ROWENA. He didn't look like he was rough and nasty.

LINDA. He's not rough and nasty. He just—suffers.

ROWENA. I know 'em.

LINDA. Aunt Rowena, isn't there any way discovered to make a man get over loving you. Can it be cured?

Rowena *does not answer. She walks meditatively back to the table in the corner.*

ROWENA. Give me a hand, will you, with this table. We'll bring it nearer to the gas jet. I'd better go downstairs and see what Joey's doing to

everything. (*They bring the table forward.*)
Dearie, what makes you say such things? What
makes you say he's thinking of shooting you?

LINDA. He looked all . . . all crazy and said I
oughtn't to be alive. He said if I didn't marry
him . . .

ROWENA. *Marry him!* He asked you to marry
him? Linda, you are a funny girl not to tell me
these things before. Why do you keep everything
so secret, dearie?

LINDA. I didn't think that was a secret. I don't
want to marry him.

ROWENA (*passing her thumb along her teeth
and looking at* Linda *narrowly*). Well, now try
and remember what he said about shooting.

LINDA. He was standing at the door saying
goodbye. I was playing with the key in my hand
to show him I was in a hurry to be done with him.
He said he couldn't think of anything but me—
that he couldn't live without me and so on. Then
he asked me was there someone else I loved instead of him, and I said no. And he said how
about the Italian fellow at Madame Angellelli's
swarray, and I said no, not in a thousand years. He
meant Mario. And then he started to cry and take
on terrible.—Imagine being jealous of Mario.

ROWENA. I'll teach that young man a lesson.
That's what I'll do.

LINDA. Then he was trembling all over, and he
took up the edge of my coat and cried: People

like me ought not to be alive. Nature ought not
to allow such soulless beauties like I.

She has risen on her toes, holding out her
arms and has started drifting away with little
rapid steps. From the back of the stage she
calls scornfully:

I ought not to be alive, he said. I ought not to
be alive.

Pause.

ROWENA. Someone's pounding on the street
door down there. Joey must have dropped the
latch.

LINDA. It's Arthur.

ROWENA. Don't be foolish.

LINDA. I know in my bones it's him.

Joey *appears at the back.*

JOEY. There's a gentleman to see you, Linda.
Says his name is Warburton.

LINDA. Yes. Send him up.

JOEY. Kipper is almost ready. Water's boiling,
Rowena. What are you going to do about this
visitor?

ROWENA. Listen dearie, I want to look at this
Arthur again. You ask him pretty to have supper
with us.

LINDA. Oh, Aunt Rowena, I couldn't eat!

ROWENA. This is serious. This is serious, Linda.
Now you ask him to supper and send him around
the corner for some bitters. In the meantime I'll
catch a minute to tell Joey how we must watch
him.

Linda. I don't care if he shoots me. It's nothing to me.

In the gloom at the back Arthur *appears. He is wearing an opera hat and cape.*

Arthur (*he is very miserable. He expects and dreads* Linda's *indifference but hopes that some miraculous change of heart may occur any minute. Tentatively*). Good evening, Linda.

Linda. Hello, Arthur. Arthur, I'd like you to meet my aunt, Mrs. Rowena Stoker.

Arthur. It's a great pleasure to meet you, Mrs. Stoker. I hope I'm not intruding. I was just passing by and I thought . . . (*his voice trails off*)

Rowena. We thought there was going to be a rehearsal of the new panto we're engaged for, Mr. Warburton. But nobody's showed up so like as not we mistook the day. Linda's just been practicing a few steps for practice, haven't you, dovie?

Linda (*by rote*). Arthur, we were just going to have a little supper. We hope you'll have some with us. Just a kippered herring and some tea.

Arthur. That's awfully good of you. I've just come from dinner. But I hope you won't mind if I sit by you, Mrs. Stoker.

Rowena. Suit yourself, I always say. It isn't very attractive in an empty theatre. But you must have something, oh yes.

Linda. Perhaps you'd like to do us a favor, Arthur. Joey's downstairs doing the cooking and can't go. Perhaps you'd like to go down to the corner and bring us a jug of ale and bitters.

Rowena. I have a shilling here somewhere.

Linda. Aunt Rowena, perhaps Arthur is dressed too grand to go to a pub. . . .

Rowena. The pubs in this street is used to us coming in in all kinds of costumes, Mr. Warburton. They'll think you're rehearsing for a society play.

Arthur (*who has refused the shilling, and is all feverish willingness*). I'll be right back. I'll only be a minute, Mrs. Stoker.

He hurries out.

Rowena. The poor boy is off his head for fair. Makes me feel all *old* just to see him. But I imagine he's quite a nice young man when he's got his senses. But never mind, Linda, nobody wants you to marry anybody you don't want to marry.— Has he been drinking, dearie, or does he just look that way?

Linda. He just looks that way.

Enter Joey, with cups, knives, forks, etc.

Joey. Where's the duke?

Rowena. He's gone to the corner for some ale and bitters. Thank God, he's eaten already. Now Joey, listen. This young man is off his head about Linda, crazy for fair. Now this is serious. Linda says he talks wild and might even be thinking of shooting her. (Joey *whistles.*) Well, the papers are full of such things, Joey. And plays are full of it. It might be. It might be.

Joey. Well, I've heard about such things, but it never happened in my family.

ROWENA. Just the same we must take steps. Joey, I'll have him take his cape off. You take it downstairs and see if there's anything in the pocket.

JOEY. What in the pocket?

ROWENA. Why . . . one of those small guns.

LINDA. Yes, of course, there's one in his pocket. I know there is.

ROWENA. It would be in his cape so as not to bulge his other pockets. Listen, Joey, if there is a gun there, you take out the bullets, and then put the gun back into his pocket empty. See? Then bring the cape back again. If this boy is going to shoot Linda, he's going to shoot her tonight, so we can have a good heart-to-heart talk about it.

JOEY. Yes, and then call the police, that's what!

ROWENA. No, this is a thing police and prisons can't cure. Now, Joey, if you find a gun in his pocket and have done what I told you, you come back on the stage whistling one of your songs. Whistle your song about Bank holidays. You know: *My holiday girl on a holiday bus.*

JOEY. Right-o!

ROWENA. Now, Linda, you act just natural. Let him have his murder and get it out of his system. Yes, you know I like the boy and I don't hold it against him. When we're twenty-one years old we all have a few drops of crazy melodrama in us.

LINDA (*suddenly*). Oh, I hate him, I 'ate 'im! Why can't he let me be?

ROWENA. Yes, yes. That's love.

LINDA (*on the verge of hysterics*). Auntie, can't it be cured? Can't you make him just forget me?

ROWENA. Well, dovie, they say there are some ways. Some say you can make fun of him and mock him out of it. And some say you can show yourself up at your worst or pretend you're worse than you are. But I say there's only one way to cure that kind of love when it's feverish and all upset.

She pauses groping for her thought.

Only love can cure love. Only being interested . . . only being real interested and fond of him can . . . can . . .

She gives it up.

It's all right, dearie. Don't you get jumpy. It's a lucky chance to get the thing cleared up. Only remember this: I like him. I like him. He's just somebody's boy that's not well for a few weeks.

LINDA. He breathes too hard.

Enter Arthur, *followed by* Joey. Arthur's *hands are laden with bundles and bottles.*

ROWENA. Why, Mr. Warburton, I never see such a load. Whatever did you find to bring? Fries? Salami, and I don't know what all. This *is* a feast. Take off your coat, Mr. Warburton. Joey, help Mr. Warburton off with his coat. Take it and hang it on the peg downstairs.

ARTHUR. (*with concern*). I think I'll keep the coat, thanks.

ROWENA (*as* Joey *attacks it*). Oh, no, no! You won't need your coat. There's nothing worse than sitting about in a heavy coat.

Arthur *follows it with his eyes, as* Joey *bears it off.*

But Linda, you've been exercising. You slip that scarf about you, dearie, and draw up your chair. Well, this is going to be nice. What's nicer than friends sitting down to a bite to eat? And extra nice for you, Mr. Warburton, because you ought to be in your university, or am I mistaken?

ARTHUR. Yes, I ought to be at Cambridge.

ROWENA. Fancy that! It must be exciting to break the rule so boldly. Ah, well, life is so dull that it does us good every now and then to *make* a little excitement. Now, Mr. Warburton, you'll change your mind and have a little snack with us. A slice of Salami?

ARTHUR. I don't think I could eat anything. I'll have a little ale.

ROWENA (*busying herself over the table*). That's right.

ARTHUR (*ventures a word to* Linda). Madame Angellelli is having a soirée Thursday, Linda. Don't you go any more?

LINDA. No, I don't like them.

ARTHUR. I wondered where you were last Thursday. Madame Angellelli expected you every minute.

LINDA. I don't like them.

Silence.

ROWENA. What can be keeping Joey over the kipper? Have you seen Joey on the stage, Mr. Warburton?—Joey Weston he is.

ARTHUR. No, I don't think I have.

ROWENA. Oh, very fine, he is! Quite the best comedian in the pantos. But surely you must have seen his wife. She was Henrietta du Vaux. She was the most popular soubrette in all England, and very famous, she was. He lost her two years ago, Henrietta du Vaux. Everybody loved her. It was a terrible loss. Sh—here he comes!

> *Enter* Joey *with the kipper and the tea. He is jubilantly whistling a tune that presently breaks out into the words:* "A holiday girl on a holiday bus."

What a noise you do make, Joey, for fair. Anybody'd think you were happy about something. Well, now, Mr. Warburton, you'll excuse us if we sit down and fall right to.

> Arthur *sits at the left turned toward them.* Joey *faces the audience, with* Rowena *and* Linda *facing one another,* Rowena *at his right and* Linda *at his left.*

JOEY. It's cold here, Rowena, after the kitchen.

ROWENA. Yes, it's colder than I thought for. Joey, go and get Mr. Warburton's coat for him. I think he'll want it after all.

ARTHUR. Yes, I'd better keep it by me.

He follows Joey *to the door and takes the coat from him.*

ROWENA (*while the men are at the door*). How do you feel, dearie?

LINDA. I hate it. I wish I were home.

ROWENA. Joey, this is good. You're a good cook.

They eat absorbedly for a few moments; then Rowena *gazes out into the vault of the dark theatre.*

Oh, this old theatre has seen some wonderful nights! I'll never forget you, Joey, in *Robinson Crusoe the Second*. I'll never forget you standing right there and pretending you saw a ghost. I hurt myself laughing.

JOEY. No, it wasn't me. It was Henrietta. She sang *The Sultan of Bagdad* three hundred times in this very house. On these very same boards. Three hundred times the house went crazy when she sang *The Houseboat Song*. They'd sit so quiet you'd think they were holding their breaths, and then they'd break out into shouts and cries. Henrietta du Vaux was my wife, Mr. Warburton. She was the best soubrette in England since Nell Gwynne, sir.

ROWENA. I can hear her now, Joey. She was as good a friend as she was a singer.

JOEY. After the show I would be waiting for her at the corner, Mr. Warburton. (*He points to the corner.*) Do you know the corner, sir?

ARTHUR (*fascinated*). Yes.

Joey. I did not always have an engagement and the manager did not think it right to have a husband waiting in the theatre to take the soubrette home. So I waited for her at that corner. She slipped away from all that applause, sir, to go home with a husband that did not always have an engagement.

Rowena. Joey, I won't have you saying that. You're one of the best comics in England.—Joey, you're tired. Rest yourself a bit.

Joey. No, Rowena, I want to say this about her: She never felt her success. And she had a hundred ways of pretending that she was no success at all. "Joey," she'd say, "I got it all wrong tonight." And then she'd ask me how she should do it.

Rowena. Do draw up a chair, Mr. Warburton, and have a bite for good feelings' sake. We're all friends here. Linda, put a piece of sausage on some bread for him, with your own hands.

Arthur. Well, thanks, thank you very much.

Joey (*with increasing impressiveness*). And when she was ill, she knew that her coughing hurt me. And she'd suffer four times over trying to hold back her coughing. "Cough, Henrietta," I'd say, "if it makes you more comfortable." But no!— she'd act like I was the sick person that had to be taken care of.

Turning on Arthur *with gravity and force.*

I read in the papers about people who shoot the persons they love. I don't know what to think.

What is it but that they want to be *noticed,* noticed even if they must shoot to get noticed? It's themselves—it's themselves they love.

> Joey *stares at* Arthur *so fixedly that* Arthur *breathes an all but involuntary "Yes." Then he rises abruptly and says:*

Arthur. I must go now. You've been very kind.

Rowena (*rising*). Joey, come downstairs with me a minute and help me open that old chest. I think we can find Henrietta's shield and spear from *The Palace of Ice* and other things. The lock's been broken for years.

Joey. All right, Rowena. Let's look.

Rowena. We won't be a minute. You go on eating.

> *They go out.*

Arthur. I won't trouble you any more, Linda. I want you to be happy, that's all.

Linda. You don't trouble me, Arthur.

Arthur. What he said is true. I want to be noticed. I wish you liked me, Linda. I mean I wish you liked me more. I wish I could prove to you that I'd do anything for you. That I could bring to you all . . . that that he was describing. . . . I won't be a trouble to you any more. (*He turns*) I can prove it to you, Linda. I've been waiting at that corner for hours, just walking up and down. And I'd planned, Linda, to prove that I couldn't live without you, . . . and if you were going to be cold and . . . didn't like me, Linda, I was going to shoot myself right here . . . to prove to you.

He puts the revolver on the table.

To prove to you.—But you've all been so kind to me. And that . . . and Mr. Weston told about his wife. I think just loving isn't wasted.

He weeps silently.

LINDA (*horrified*). Arthur! I wish you wouldn't!

ARTHUR. I imagine I'm . . . I'm young still.— Goodbye and thanks. Goodbye.

He hurries out.

Linda shudders with distaste; peers at the revolver; starts to walk about the room and presently is sketching steps again.

Joey *and* Rowena *return.*

ROWENA. Was that he that went out? What happened, Linda?

LINDA (*interrupting her drill, indifferently*). He said goodbye forever. He left the gun to prove to me something or other. Thank you for nothing.

ROWENA. Linda, I hope you said a nice word to him.

LINDA. Thank you for nothing, I said.

ROWENA. Well, young lady, you're only sixteen. Wait 'til your turn comes. We'll have to take care of you.

LINDA. Don't let's talk about it. It makes me tired. So hot and excited and breathing so hard. Mario would never act like that. Mario . . . Mario doesn't even seem to notice you when you're there. . . .

And the curtain falls.

The Happy Journey to Trenton and Camden

No scenery is required for this play. Perhaps a few dusty flats may be seen leaning against the brick wall at the back of the stage.

The five members of the Kirby family and the Stage Manager *compose the cast.*

The Stage Manager *not only moves forward and withdraws the few properties that are required, but he reads from a typescript the lines of all the minor characters. He reads them clearly, but with little attempt at characterization, scarcely troubling himself to alter his voice, even when he responds in the person of a child or a woman.*

As the curtain rises the Stage Manager *is leaning lazily against the proscenium pillar at the audience's left. He is smoking.*

Arthur *is playing marbles in the center of the stage.*

Caroline *is at the remote back right talking to some girls who are invisible to us.*

Ma Kirby *is anxiously putting on her hat before an imaginary mirror.*

MA. Where's your pa? Why isn't he here? I declare we'll never get started.

ARTHUR. Ma, where's my hat? I guess I don't go if I can't find my hat.

MA. Go out into the hall and see if it isn't there. Where's Caroline gone to now, the plagued child?

ARTHUR. She's out waitin' in the street talkin' to the Jones girls.—I just looked in the hall a thousand times, ma, and it isn't there. (*He spits for good luck before a difficult shot and mutters:*) Come on, baby.

MA. Go and look again, I say. Look carefully.

Arthur *rises, runs to the right, turns around swiftly, returns to his game, flinging himself on the floor with a terrible impact and starts shooting an aggie.*

ARTHUR. No, ma, it's not there.

MA (*serenely*). Well, you don't leave Newark without that hat, make up your mind to that. I don't go no journeys with a hoodlum.

ARTHUR. Aw, ma!

Ma *comes down to the footlights and talks toward the audience as through a window.*

MA. Oh, Mrs. Schwartz!

THE STAGE MANAGER (*consulting his script*). Here I am, Mrs. Kirby. Are you going yet?

MA. I guess we're going in just a minute. How's the baby?

THE STAGE MANAGER. She's all right now. We slapped her on the back and she spat it up.

MA. Isn't that fine!—Well now, if you'll be good enough to give the cat a saucer of milk in the morning and the evening, Mrs. Schwartz, I'll be ever so grateful to you.—Oh, good afternoon, Mrs. Hobmeyer!

THE STAGE MANAGER. Good afternoon, Mrs. Kirby, I hear you're going away.

MA (*modest*). Oh, just for three days, Mrs. Hobmeyer, to see my married daughter, Beulah, in Camden. Elmer's got his vacation week from the laundry early this year, and he's just the best driver in the world.

Caroline *comes "into the house" and stands by her mother.*

THE STAGE MANAGER. Is the whole family going?

MA. Yes, all four of us that's here. The change ought to be good for the children. My married daughter was downright sick a while ago—

THE STAGE MANAGER. Tchk—Tchk—Tchk! Yes. I remember you tellin' us.

MA. And I just want to go down and see the child. I ain't seen her since then. I just won't rest easy in my mind without I see her. (*To Caroline*) Can't you say good afternoon to Mrs. Hobmeyer?

CAROLINE (*blushes and lowers her eyes and says woodenly*). Good afternoon, Mrs. Hobmeyer.

THE STAGE MANAGER. Good afternoon, dear.— Well, I'll wait and beat these rugs until after you're gone, because I don't want to choke you. I hope you have a good time and find everything all right.

MA. Thank you, Mrs. Hobmeyer, I hope I will.

—Well, I guess that milk for the cat is all, Mrs. Schwartz, if you're sure you don't mind. If anything should come up, the key to the back door is hanging by the ice box.

ARTHUR AND CAROLINE. Ma! Not so loud. Everybody can hear yuh.

MA. Stop pullin' my dress, children. (*In a loud whisper*) The key to the back door I'll leave hangin' by the ice box and I'll leave the screen door unhooked.

THE STAGE MANAGER. Now have a good trip, dear, and give my love to Loolie.

MA. I will, and thank you a thousand times.

She returns "into the room."

What can be keeping your pa?

ARTHUR. I can't find my hat, ma.

Enter Elmer *holding a hat.*

ELMER. Here's Arthur's hat. He musta left it in the car Sunday.

MA. That's a mercy. Now we can start.—Caroline Kirby, what you done to your cheeks?

CAROLINE (*defiant-abashed*). Nothin'.

MA. If you've put anything on 'em, I'll slap you.

CAROLINE. No, ma, of course I haven't. (*hanging her head*) I just rubbed'm to make'm red. All the girls do that at High School when they're goin' places.

MA. Such silliness I never saw. Elmer, what kep' you?

ELMER (*always even-voiced and always looking*

out a little anxiously through his spectacles). I just went to the garage and had Charlie give a last look at it, Kate.

MA. I'm glad you did. I wouldn't like to have no breakdown miles from anywhere. Now we can start. Arthur, put those marbles away. Anybody'd think you didn't want to go on a journey to look at yuh.

They go out through the "hall," take the short steps that denote going downstairs, and find themselves in the street.

ELMER. Here, you boys, you keep away from that car.

MA. Those Sullivan boys put their heads into everything.

The Stage Manager *has moved forward four chairs and a low platform. This is the automobile. It is in the center of the stage and faces the audience. The platform slightly raises the two chairs in the rear. Pa's hands hold an imaginary steering wheel and continually shift gears.* Caroline *sits beside him.* Arthur *is behind him and* Ma *behind* Caroline.

CAROLINE (*self-consciously*). Goodbye, Mildred. Goodbye, Helen.

THE STAGE MANAGER. Goodbye, Caroline. Goodbye, Mrs. Kirby. I hope y'have a good time.

MA. Goodbye, girls.

THE STAGE MANAGER. Goodbye, Kate. The car looks fine.

MA. (*looking upward toward a window*). Oh, goodbye, Emma! (*modestly*) We think it's the best little Chevrolet in the world.—Oh, goodbye, Mrs. Adler!

THE STAGE MANAGER. What, are you going away, Mrs. Kirby?

MA. Just for three days, Mrs. Adler, to see my married daughter in Camden.

THE STAGE MANAGER. Have a good time.

> *Now* Ma, Caroline, *and the* Stage Manager *break out into a tremendous chorus of goodbyes. The whole street is saying goodbye.* Arthur *takes out his pea shooter and lets fly happily into the air. There is a lurch or two and they are off.*

ARTHUR (*in sudden fright*). Pa! Pa! Don't go by the school. Mr. Biedenbach might see us!

MA. I don't care if he does see us. I guess I can take my children out of school for one day without having to hide down back streets about it.

> Elmer *nods to a passerby.*

> Ma *asks without sharpness:*

Who was that you spoke to, Elmer?

ELMER. That was the fellow who arranges our banquets down to the Lodge, Kate.

MA. Is he the one who had to buy four hundred steaks? (Pa *nods.*) I declare, I'm glad I'm not him.

ELMER. The air's getting better already. Take deep breaths, children.

> *They inhale noisily.*

ARTHUR. Gee, it's almost open fields already. *"Weber and Heilbronner Suits for Well-dressed Men."* Ma, can I have one of them some day?

MA. If you graduate with good marks perhaps your father'll let you have one for graduation.

CAROLINE (*whining*). Oh, Pa! do we have to wait while that whole funeral goes by?

Pa *takes off his hat.*

Ma *cranes forward with absorbed curiosity.*

MA. Take off your hat, Arthur. Look at your father.—Why, Elmer, I do believe that's a lodge-brother of yours. See the banner? I suppose this is the Elizabeth branch.

Elmer *nods.* Ma *sighs: Tchk—tchk—tchk. They all lean forward and watch the funeral in silence, growing momentarily more solemnized. After a pause,* Ma *continues almost dreamily:*

Well, we haven't forgotten the one that we went on, have we? We haven't forgotten our good Harold. He gave his life for his country, we mustn't forget that. (*She passes her finger from the corner of her eye across her cheek. There is another pause.*) Well, we'll all hold up the traffic for a few minutes some day.

THE CHILDREN (*very uncomfortable*). Ma!

MA. (*without self-pity*). Well I'm "ready," children. I hope everybody in this car is "ready." (*She puts her hand on* Pa's *shoulder.*) And I pray to go first, Elmer. Yes. (Pa *touches her hand.*)

THE CHILDREN. Ma, everybody's looking at you. Everybody's laughing at you.

MA. Oh, hold your tongues! I don't care what a lot of silly people in Elizabeth, New Jersey, think of me.—Now we can go on. That's the last.

There is another lurch and the car goes on.

CAROLINE. *"Fit-Rite Suspenders. The Working Man's Choice."* Pa, why do they spell Rite that way?

ELMER. So that it'll make you stop and ask about it, Missy.

CAROLINE. Papa, you're teasing me.—Ma, why do they say *"Three Hundred Rooms Three Hundred Baths?"*

ARTHUR. *"Miller's Spaghetti: The Family's Favorite Dish."* Ma, why don't you ever have spaghetti?

MA. Go along, you'd never eat it.

ARTHUR. Ma, I like it now.

CAROLINE (*with gesture*). Yum-yum. It looks wonderful up there. Ma, make some when we get home?

MA. (*dryly*). "The management is always happy to receive suggestions. We aim to please."

The whole family finds this exquisitely funny. The children scream with laughter. Even Elmer *smiles.* Ma *remains modest.*

ELMER. Well, I guess no one's complaining, Kate. Everybody knows you're a good cook.

MA. I don't know whether I'm a good cook or

not, but I know I've had practice. At least I've cooked three meals a day for twenty-five years.

ARTHUR. Aw, ma, you went out to eat once in a while.

MA. Yes. That made it a leap year.

This joke is no less successful than its prede-cessor. When the laughter dies down, Caroline *turns around in an ecstasy of well-being and kneeling on the cushions says:*

CAROLINE. Ma, I love going out in the country like this. Let's do it often, ma.

MA. Goodness, smell that air will you! It's got the whole ocean in it.—Elmer, drive careful over that bridge. This must be New Brunswick we're coming to.

ARTHUR (*jealous of his mother's successes*). Ma, when is the next comfort station?

MA. (*unruffled*). You don't want one. You just said that to be awful.

CAROLINE (*shrilly*). Yes, he did, ma. He's ter-rible. He says that kind of thing right out in school and I want to sink through the floor, ma. He's terrible.

MA. Oh, don't get so excited about nothing, Miss Proper! I guess we're all yewman-beings in this car, at least as far as I know. And, Arthur, you try and be a gentleman.—Elmer, don't run over that collie dog. (*She follows the dog with her eyes.*) Looked kinda peakèd to me. Needs a good honest bowl of leavings. Pretty dog, too. (*Her eyes fall on a billboard.*) That's a pretty advertisement for Chesterfield cigarettes, isn't it? Looks like Beulah, a little.

ARTHUR. Ma?

MA. Yes.

ARTHUR (*"route" rhymes with "out"*). Can't I take a paper route with the Newark *Daily Post?*

MA. No, you cannot. No, sir. I hear they make the paper boys get up at four-thirty in the morning. No son of mine is going to get up at four-thirty every morning, not if it's to make a million dollars. Your *Saturday Evening Post* route on Thursday mornings is enough.

ARTHUR. Aw, ma.

MA. No, sir. No son of mine is going to get up at four-thirty and miss the sleep God meant him to have.

ARTHUR (*sullenly*). Hhm! Ma's always talking about God. I guess she got a letter from him this morning.

Ma *rises, outraged.*

MA. Elmer, stop that automobile this minute. I don't go another step with anybody that says things like that. Arthur, you get out of this car. Elmer, you give him another dollar bill. He can go back to Newark, by himself. I don't want him.

ARTHUR. What did I say? There wasn't anything terrible about that.

ELMER. I didn't hear what he said, Kate.

MA. God has done a lot of things for me and I

won't have him made fun of by anybody. Go away. Go away from me.

CAROLINE. Aw, Ma,—don't spoil the ride.

MA. No.

ELMER. We might as well go on, Kate, since we've got started. I'll talk to the boy tonight.

MA (*slowly conceding*). All right, if you say so, Elmer. But I won't sit beside him. Caroline, you come, and sit by me.

ARTHUR (*frightened*). Aw, ma, that wasn't so terrible.

MA. I don't want to talk about it. I hope your father washes your mouth out with soap and water.—Where'd we all be if I started talking about God like that, I'd like to know! We'd be in the speak-easies and night-clubs and places like that, that's where we'd be.—All right, Elmer, you can go on now.

CAROLINE. What did he say, ma? I didn't hear what he said.

MA. I don't want to talk about it.

They drive on in silence for a moment, the shocked silence after a scandal.

ELMER. I'm going to stop and give the car a little water, I guess.

MA. All right, Elmer. You know best.

ELMER (*to a garage hand*). Could I have a little water in the radiator—to make sure?

THE STAGE MANAGER (*in this scene alone he lays aside his script and enters into a rôle seri-*

ously). You sure can. (*He punches the tires.*) Air, all right? Do you need any oil or gas?

ELMER. No, I think not. I just got fixed up in Newark.

MA. We're on the right road for Camden, are we?

THE STAGE MANAGER. Yes, keep straight ahead. You can't miss it. You'll be in Trenton in a few minutes.

He carefully pours some water into the hood.

Camden's a great town, lady, believe me.

MA. My daughter likes it fine,—my married daughter.

THE STAGE MANAGER. Ye'? It's a great burg all right. I guess I think so because I was born near there.

MA. Well, well. Your folks still live there?

THE STAGE MANAGER. No, my old man sold the farm and they built a factory on it. So the folks moved to Philadelphia.

MA. My married daughter Beulah lives there because her husband works in the telephone company.—Stop pokin' me, Caroline!—We're all going down to see her for a few days.

THE STAGE MANAGER. Ye'?

MA. She's been sick, you see, and I just felt I had to go and see her. My husband and my boy are going to stay at the Y.M.C.A. I hear they've got a dormitory on the top floor that's real clean and comfortable. Had you ever been there?

THE STAGE MANAGER. No. I'm Knights of Columbus myself.

MA. Oh.

THE STAGE MANAGER. I used to play basketball at the Y though. It looked all right to me.

He has been standing with one foot on the rung of Ma's *chair. They have taken a great fancy to one another. He reluctantly shakes himself out of it and pretends to examine the car again, whistling.*

Well, I guess you're all set now, lady. I hope you have a good trip; you can't miss it.

EVERYBODY. Thanks. Thanks a lot. Good luck to you.

Jolts and lurches.

MA. (*with a sigh*). The world's full of nice people.—That's what I call a nice young man.

CAROLINE (*earnestly*). Ma, you oughtn't to tell'm all everything about yourself.

MA. Well, Caroline, you do your way and I'll do mine.—He looked kinda thin to me. I'd like to feed him up for a few days. His mother lives in Philadelphia and I expect he eats at those dreadful Greek places.

CAROLINE. I'm hungry. Pa, there's a hot dog stand. K'n I have one?

ELMER. We'll all have one, eh, Kate? We had such an early lunch.

MA. Just as you think best, Elmer.

ELMER. Arthur, here's half a dollar.—Run over

and see what they have. Not too much mustard
either.

Arthur *descends from the car and goes off*
stage right.

Ma *and* Caroline *get out and walk a bit.*

MA. What's that flower over there?—I'll take
some of those to Beulah.

CAROLINE. It's just a weed, ma.

MA. I like it.—My, look at the sky, wouldya!
I'm glad I was born in New Jersey. I've always
said it was the best state in the Union. Every state
has something no other state has got.

They stroll about humming.

Presently Arthur *returns with his hands full*
of imaginary hot dogs which he distributes.
He is still very much cast down by the recent
scandal. He finally approaches his mother
and says falteringly:

ARTHUR. Ma, I'm sorry. I'm sorry for what I
said.

He bursts into tears and puts his forehead
against her elbow.

MA. There. There. We all say wicked things
at times. I know you didn't mean it like it
sounded.

He weeps still more violently than before.

Why, now, now! I forgive you, Arthur and tonight before you go to bed you . . . (*she whis-*
pers.) You're a good boy at heart, Arthur, and we
all know it.

Caroline *starts to cry too.*

Ma *is suddenly joyously alive and happy.*

Sakes alive, it's too nice a day for us all to be cryin'. Come now, get in. You go up in front with your father, Caroline. Ma wants to sit with her beau. I never saw such children. Your hot dogs are all getting wet. Now chew them fine, everybody.—All right, Elmer, forward march.—Caroline, whatever are you doing?

CAROLINE. I'm spitting out the leather, ma.

MA. Then say: Excuse me.

CAROLINE. Excuse me, please.

MA. What's this place? Arthur, did you see the post office?

ARTHUR. It said Laurenceville.

MA. Hhn. School kinda. Nice. I wonder what that big yellow house set back was.—Now it's beginning to be Trenton.

CAROLINE. Papa, it was near here that George Washington crossed the Delaware. It was near Trenton, mama. He was first in war and first in peace, and first in the hearts of his countrymen.

MA. (*surveying the passing world, serene and didactic*). Well, the thing I like about him best was that he never told a lie.

The children are duly cast down.

There is a pause.

There's a sunset for you. There's nothing like a good sunset.

ARTHUR. There's an Ohio license in front of us. Ma, have you ever been to Ohio?

MA. No.

A dreamy silence descends upon them.

Caroline *sits closer to her father.*

Ma *puts her arm around* Arthur.

ARTHUR. Ma, what a lotta people there are in the world, ma. There must be thousands and thousands in the United States. Ma, how many are there?

MA. I don't know. Ask your father.

ARTHUR. Pa, how many are there?

ELMER. There are a hundred and twenty-six million, Kate.

MA (*giving a pressure about* Arthur's *shoulder*). And they all like to drive out in the evening with their children beside'm.

Another pause.

Why doesn't somebody sing something? Arthur, you're always singing something; what's the matter with you?

ARTHUR. All right. What'll we sing? (*He sketches:*)

"In the Blue Ridge mountains of Virginia,
  On the trail of the lonesome pine . . ."

No, I don't like that any more. Let's do:

"I been workin on de railroad
  All de liblong day.
  I been workin' on de railroad
  Just to pass de time away."

Caroline *joins in at once.*

Finally even Ma *is singing.*

Even Pa *is singing.*

Ma *suddenly jumps up with a wild cry:*

MA. Elmer, that signpost said Camden, I saw it.

ELMER. All right, Kate, if you're sure.

Much shifting of gears, backing, and jolting.

MA. Yes, there it is. Camden—five miles. Dear old Beulah.—Now, children, you be good and quiet during dinner. She's just got out of bed after a big sorta operation, and we must all move around kinda quiet. First you drop me and Caroline at the door and just say hello, and then you men-folk go over to the Y.M.C.A. and come back for dinner in about an hour.

CAROLINE (*shutting her eyes and pressing her fists passionately against her nose*). I see the first star. Everybody make a wish.

Star light, star bright,

First star I seen tonight.

I wish I may, I wish I might

Have the wish I wish tonight.

(*then solemnly*) Pins. Mama, you say "needles."

She interlocks little fingers with her mother.

MA. Needles.

CAROLINE. Shakespeare. Ma, you say "Longfellow."

MA. Longfellow.

CAROLINE. Now it's a secret and I can't tell it to anybody. Ma, you make a wish.

MA. (*with almost grim humor*). No, I can make wishes without waiting for no star. And I can tell my wishes right out loud too. Do you want to hear them?

CAROLINE (*resignedly*). No, ma, we know'm already. We've heard'm. (*She hangs her head affectedly on her left shoulder and says with unmalicious mimicry:*) You want me to be a good girl and you want Arthur to be honest-in-word-and-deed.

MA. (*majestically*). Yes. So mind yourself.

ELMER. Caroline, take out that letter from Beulah in my coat pocket by you and read aloud the places I marked with red pencil.

CAROLINE (*working*). "*A few blocks after you pass the two big oil tanks on your left . . .*"

EVERYBODY (*pointing backward*). There they are!

CAROLINE. "*. . . you come to a corner where there's an A and P store on the left and a firehouse kitty-corner to it . . .*"

They all jubilantly identify these landmarks. "*. . . turn right, go two blocks, and our house is Weyerhauser St. Number 471.*"

MA. It's an even nicer street than they used to live in. And right handy to an A and P.

CAROLINE (*whispering*). Ma, it's better than our street. It's richer than our street.—Ma, isn't Beulah richer than we are?

MA. (*looking at her with a firm and glassy eye*). Mind yourself, missy. I don't want to hear anybody talking about rich or not rich when I'm around. If people aren't nice I don't care how rich they are. I live in the best street in the world because my husband and children live there.

She glares impressively at Caroline *a moment to let this lesson sink in, then looks up, sees* Beulah *and waves.*

There's Beulah standing on the steps lookin' for us.

Beulah *has appeared and is waving.*

They all call out: Hello, Beulah—Hello.

Presently they are all getting out of the car. Beulah *kisses her father long and affectionately.*

BEULAH. Hello, papa. Good old papa. You look tired, pa.—Hello, mama.—Lookit how Arthur and Caroline are growing!

MA. They're bursting all their clothes!—Yes, your pa needs a rest. Thank Heaven, his vacation has come just now. We'll feed him up and let him sleep late. Pa has a present for you, Loolie. He would go and buy it.

BEULAH. Why, pa, you're terrible to go and buy anything for me. Isn't he terrible?

MA. Well, it's a secret. You can open it at dinner.

ELMER. Where's Horace, Loolie?

BEULAH. He was kep' over a little at the office. He'll be here any minute. He's crazy to see you all.

MA. All right. You men go over to the Y and come back in about an hour.

BEULAH (*as her father returns to the wheel, stands out in the street beside him*). Go straight along, pa, you can't miss it. It just stares at yuh.

(*She puts her arm around his neck and rubs her nose against his temple.*) Crazy old pa, goin' buyin' things! It's me that ought to be buyin' things for you, pa.

ELMER. Oh, no! There's only one Loolie in the world.

BEULAH (*whispering, as her eyes fill with tears*). Are you glad I'm still alive, pa?

> *She kisses him abruptly and goes back to the house steps.*
>
> The Stage Manager *removes the automobile with the help of* Elmer *and* Arthur *who go off waving their goodbyes.*

Well, come on upstairs, ma, and take off your things.

Caroline, there's a surprise for you in the back yard.

CAROLINE. Rabbits?

BEULAH. No.

CAROLINE. Chickins?

BEULAH. No. Go and see.

> Caroline *runs off stage.*
>
> Beulah *and* Ma *gradually go upstairs.*

There are two new puppies. You be thinking over whether you can keep one in Newark.

MA. I guess we can. It's a nice house, Beulah. You just got a *lovely* home.

BEULAH. When I got back from the hospital, Horace had moved everything into it, and there wasn't anything for me to do.

MA. It's lovely.

The Stage Manager *pushes out a bed from the left. Its foot is toward the right. Beulah sits on it, testing the springs.*

BEULAH. I think you'll find the bed comfortable, ma.

MA (*taking off her hat*). Oh, I could sleep on a heapa shoes, Loolie! I don't have no trouble sleepin'. (*She sits down beside her.*) Now let me look at my girl. Well, well, when I last saw you, you didn't know me. You kep' saying: *When's mama comin'? When's mama comin'?* But the doctor sent me away.

BEULAH (*puts her head on her mother's shoulder and weeps*). It was awful, mama. It was awful. She didn't even live a few minutes, mama. It was awful.

MA (*looking far away*). God thought best, dear. God thought best. We don't understand why. We just go on, honey, doin' our business.

Then almost abruptly—passing the back of her hand across her cheek.

Well, now, what are we giving the men to eat tonight?

BEULAH. There's a chicken in the oven.

MA. What time didya put it in?

BEULAH (*restraining her*). Aw, ma, don't go yet. I like to sit here with you this way. You always get the fidgets when we try and pet yuh, mama.

MA. (*ruefully, laughing*). Yes, it's kinda foolish. I'm just an old Newark bag-a-bones. (*She glances at the backs of her hands.*)

BEULAH (*indignantly*). Why, ma, you're good-lookin'! We always said you were good-lookin'.—And besides, you're the best ma we could ever have.

MA (*uncomfortable*). Well, I hope you like me. There's nothin' like being liked by your family.—Now I'm going downstairs to look at the chicken. You stretch out here for a minute and shut your eyes.—Have you got everything laid in for breakfast before the shops close?

BEULAH. Oh, you know! Ham and eggs.

They both laugh.

MA. I declare I never could understand what men see in ham and eggs. I think they're horrible.—What time did you put the chicken in?

BEULAH. Five o'clock.

MA. Well, now, you shut your eyes for ten minutes.

Beulah *stretches out and shuts her eyes.*

Ma *descends the stairs absent-mindedly singing:*

"There were ninety and nine that safely lay
   In the shelter of the fold,
   But one was out on the hills away,
   Far off from the gates of gold. . . ."

And the curtain falls.

Selected Bibliography

WORKS BY THORNTON WILDER

The Cabala, a novel, published in 1926.

The Bridge of San Luis Rey, a novel, published in 1927.

The Angel That Troubled the Waters, a collection of three-minute-long one-act plays primarily for reading, published in 1928.

The Woman of Andros, a novel, published in 1930.

The Long Christmas Dinner and Other Plays in One Act, a collection of one-act plays intended for the stage, published in 1931. Note: The title play in this collection was turned into a libretto by the author (translated into German by P. Hindemith) for an opera with a score by Paul Hindemith; premiere at Mannheim, Germany, on December 20, 1961.

Lucrece, a translation of André Obey's play, produced in 1932, published in 1933.

Heaven's My Destination, a novel, published in 1935.

Our Town, a play produced in 1938—first performance at Princeton, New Jersey, on January 22, published in 1938.

The Merchant of Yonkers, a play adapted from an Austrian farce by Johann Nestroy, *Einen Jux Will Er Sich Machen* (Vienna, 1842), which was in turn based upon an English original, *A Day Well Spent* (London, 1835), by John Oxenford—first performance at Boston on December 12, 1938, published in 1939.

The Skin of Our Teeth, a play produced in 1942—first performance at New Haven, Conn., on October 15, published in December 1942.

The Ides of March, a novel, published in 1948.

The Matchmaker, a revised version of *The Merchant of Yonkers,* produced in New York in 1956—performed at

Edinburgh, Scotland, August 23, 1954; first American performance at Philadelphia on October 27, 1955.

Three Plays: Preface, *Our Town, The Skin of Our Teeth,* and *The Matchmaker,* published in one volume, Harper & Brothers, 1957.

A Life in the Sun (The Alcestiad), a play produced at the Edinburgh Festival in the summer of 1955. Not yet published in English—first German-language production in 1957 in Zurich, Switzerland. Turned into a libretto by the author for an opera, with music by Louise Talma, given in German as *Die Alkestiade;* world premiere at Frankfurt-am-Main, Germany, on March 2, 1962.

Plays for Bleecker Street, three short plays *(Infancy, Childhood,* and *Someone from Assisi)*—first performance at the Circle-in-the-Square Theatre in New York on January 11, 1962.

WRITINGS ON THORNTON WILDER

ARTICLES:

"An Obliging Man," *Time* magazine, Jan. 12, 1953, pp. 44-49.

Malcolm Cowley, "The Man Who Abolished Time," *Saturday Review,* Oct. 6, 1956, pp. 13-14, 50-52.

Edmund Fuller, "Reappraisals: Thornton Wilder," *The American Scholar,* Spring 1959, pp. 210-17.

Tyrone Guthrie, "The World of Thornton Wilder," *New York Times Magazine,* November 27, 1955, pp. 26-27, 64, 66-68.

Barnard Hewitt, "Thornton Wilder Says 'Yes,' " *Tulane Drama Review,* December 1959.

Dayton Kohler, "Thornton Wilder," *English Journal,* January 1939, pp. 1-11.

Winfeld Townley Scott, "*Our Town* and the Golden

Veil," *Virginia Quarterly Review,* January 1953, pp. 103-17.

BOOKS:

Rex Burbank, *Thornton Wilder,* Twayne Publishers, 1961—the most complete study of Wilder's writings to date. (Some of the dates in the Chronology need correction.)

Francis Fergusson, *The Human Image in Dramatic Literature,* Doubleday Anchor Books, 1957. See the chapter "Three Allegorists: Brecht, Wilder and Eliot," pp. 41-71.

J.G.